MYSELF AND OTHER
MORE IMPORTANT MATTERS

Also by Elizabeth and Charles Handy

The New Alchemists
Reinvented Lives

Also by Charles Handy

Understanding Organisations
Understanding Schools as Organisations
Inside Organisations
The Age of Unreason
Gods of Management
Waiting for the Mountain to Move
The Empty Raincoat
Beyond Certainty
Thoughts for the Day
The Hungry Spirit
The Elephant and the Flea

Also by Elizabeth Handy

Behind the View
A Journey Through Tea

MYSELF AND OTHER MORE IMPORTANT MATTERS

Charles Handy

∱AMACOM

American Management Association

New York • Atlanta • Brussels • Chicago • Mexico City • San Francisco
Shanghai • Tokyo • Toronto • Washington, D.C.

Special discounts on bulk quantities of AMACOM books are available to corporations, professional associations, and other organizations. For details, contact Special Sales Department, AMACOM, a division of American Management Association, 1601 Broadway, New York, NY 10019.
Tel.: 212-903-8316.   Fax: 212-903-8083.
E-mail: specialsls@amanet.org
Website: www.amacombooks.org/go/specialsales
To view all AMACOM titles, go to www.amacombooks.org

This publication is designed to provide accurate and authoritative information in regard to the subject matter covered. It is sold with the understanding that the publisher is not engaged in rendering legal, accounting, or other professional service. If legal advice or other expert assistance is required, the services of a competent professional person should be sought.

Library of Congress Cataloging-in-Publication Data

Handy, Charles B.
    Myself and other more important matters / Charles Handy. — 1st U.S. ed.
        p.   cm.
    "Original edition published by William Heinemann, [c2006]."
    ISBN-13: 978-0-8144-0173-6
    ISBN-10: 0-8144-0173-2
    1. Handy, Charles B.   2. Business economists—Great Britain—Biography.
    3. Social scientists—Great Britain—Biography.   I. Title.

    H59.H353A3 2008
    658.0092—dc22
    [B]
                                    2007041795

Original edition published by William Heinemann, The Random House Group Limited, 20 Vauxhill Bridge Road, London SW1V 2SA.

First U.S. edition published by AMACOM, a division of American Management Association, 1601 Broadway, New York, NY 10019

Printing number

10   9   8   7   6   5   4   3   2   1

Contents

To My American Readers

My love affair with America began in 1966 when I came to the Sloan School at MIT to study for a Master's degree in Management. The London Business School, one of the first two proper business schools in Britain, had just opened its doors in a set of temporary offices above a bank. I had been recruited from the Shell Oil Company to design and run the main program for practising executives and had been sent to America to find out how such things were done. It said a lot about our two countries, I reflected, that we should be over half a century behind our American cousins in treating management as a professional discipline. Indeed, both Oxford and Cambridge had turned down the invitation from British business to provide a home for the new business schools, commenting that 'trade schools' as they termed them, had no place inside their hallowed walls.

America, in those days, was still an undiscovered country for many people in Europe. Still reeling from the after-effects of World War II, we looked with envy and admiration to the abundance that you all seemed to enjoy, to the efficiency of your businesses, to your self-confidence and your spirit of optimism, the feeling that everything was possible, no problem too difficult, even walking on the moon. It was a mood that would soon be dented by the experience of Vietnam, but this was 1966. I just hoped that a little of all that exuberance would rub off on me and that I could, in my turn, bring some of it back to my new job in London.

I found America to be wonderfully liberating. Whereas in Britain I only had to walk into a room and open my mouth for people to put me in some sort of social box, Americans seemed much more ready to take you as they found you, without enquiring or worrying about where you came from, who your parents were or where you went to school. Of course, the English accent helped. It was, it seemed, still unusual and excused all sorts of faux pas. 'Oh, that's so great', people would say, 'please say some more.' Not, I soon realised, because they were interested in what I said, just the way I said it. The new freedom meant that my wife and I could reinvent ourselves, try out new ways of thinking and behaving, with no-one to say that they weren't fooled by our new selves. Everyone, I started saying, should go and work in another country for a while, particularly if it was one as welcoming as we found America.

Of course, it was Boston where we first landed. 'When are you going to visit America?' one rather jaundiced Californian asked. America, I soon realised, was a land of many countries, all different but all miraculously held together by a cultural glue, the belief that life was what you made of it, that you alone were responsible for your destiny, which could be anything that you decided upon. In material terms it was, I discovered, a surprisingly unequal society, but, equally surprising to me, there was no serious socialist party or seemingly any desire for one. If you did not like your situation in life you only had yourself to blame, and only you could do something about it. The immigrant dream, the promise of untapped lands and endless possibilities, still lived on, even after three or four generations. It was a wonderfully robust attitude, one very different to the dependency society I had left behind.

It wasn't all roses, of course. There were drawbacks to the pioneering culture. Colleagues were also competitors and competition had its hard edge. It wasn't comfortable to be a loser in this land of opportunity. Neighbours were kind but they tended, I noticed, to help those who first helped themselves. People scorned the so-called nationalized health service of Britain, seeing it as some sort of sop for weaklings, but, personally, I always felt relieved, if only for medical reasons, when my plane touched down at Heathrow. At least they wouldn't ask for my credit card first if I got a heart attack.

And, goodness, but these Americans did work! Lunch was for wimps, it seemed, and holidays were just for kids. American capitalism, I sensed, could be exhausting. Sometimes it seemed that there wasn't too much space for the rest of life. Academics were the exception, of course. They all seemed to knock off at the end of May and go travelling around for the next three months – as I discovered when I returned to Britain and my new-found friends and colleagues came calling while we were still teaching.

I was to come back to America two or three times a year for the rest of my life. I watched it change, not always for the better I sometimes thought, but those first experiences were to be invaluable. They made me realise that there is more than one way of living, that there are different forms of capitalism, different ideas about how to run a society, or a business for that matter. Success and happiness, I realised, don't mean the same thing to everyone. You can't take anything for granted. Yes, life is what you make it, but it is not always easy to decide what sort of life it should be.

These questions have niggled at me for the rest of my life. They ultimately drove me to write this book, a book which is not so much the story of my life as the lessons that I have tried to learn from that life, often painful lessons as I came to terms with what I could not be, as well as what I could be. My hope is that my reflections may stir echoes in others and encourage them to examine their lives as I have done mine. I know now that you only learn about life by living it – reflecting on it as you go along. America set me off on that path. I still go there for an injection of energy, of that can-do attitude and for the reminder that it is, in the end, all up to me. For that I shall always be grateful.

Charles Handy
Norfolk, England

Acknowledgements

In Chekhov's play, The Seagull, the famous novelist, Trigorin, explains 'Oh yes, I love writing . . . writing is very enjoyable. Correcting proofs is very nice too. But then it's got to be published. The moment the thing is off the press I can't stand it. It's already no good, a mistake, ought never to have been written in the first place, and I feel rotten and wretched. And then people read it and they say 'oh yes, a very pretty novel . . . quite charming; but not as good as Tolstoy,' or 'a fine piece of writing, but Fathers and Sons is better.'

All writers will empathize with him. Writing a book is a lonely occupation with the final outcome always in doubt. To see one through it one needs support and encouragement at every stage. I have been fortunate to have not one, but two editors in succession at William Heinemann; Joy de Menil helped me hugely to organize my thoughts, while Caroline Knight, after Joy returned to her native America, deftly turned my drafts into the finished book and saw it through to its final resting place in the bookstores. Thereafter I know from past experience that the formidable marketing and sales teams at Random House will do their best to make sure that I don't feel too much like Trigorin. I thank them all in anticipation.

I must also thank my long-suffering family, who not only put up with the anguish of an author in their midst but who allowed me to pillage bits of their lives for this book without too much complaint. As I wrote it I realised how pivotal the family has been, and is, in my life. Elizabeth, my wife and partner, has always had more faith in my work than I have myself, which has been a great source of strength for me. I am endlessly grateful to her. I hope my appreciation of her contribution to my life is clear from the pages of this book.

Finally, as I have been writing about bits of my life I have become conscious of how many people have accompanied me on parts of my journey through life and of how much, in retrospect, I owe to them for their help along the way. I hope they know who they are, because I want to take this overdue opportunity to thank them all. My life would not have been the same without them.

Charles Handy
Norfolk and London
Spring 2006

List of Plates

Chapter One

Are You Sure?

Some years ago I was helping my wife to arrange an exhibit of her photographs of Indian tea gardens when I was approached by a man who had been looking at the pictures. 'I hear that Charles Handy is here,' he said. 'Indeed he is,' I replied, 'and I am he.' He looked at me rather dubiously for a moment, then said, 'Are you sure?' It was, I told him, a good question because over time there had been many versions of Charles Handy, not all of which I was particularly proud.

There was, for instance, the shy Anglo-Irish schoolboy born and reared in a vicarage in the Irish countryside, who, by accident, became a rather pseudo classical scholar at Oxford. There was the Shell executive who found himself struggling in the rivers and jungles of Borneo. He was trying to escape from those early influences and to enter a more exciting world, one of travel and money and power, which he imagined came with the world of business. That, I discovered, was not the Charles Handy I wanted to be. I wasn't sure for many years what that was, but the Professor Charles Handy was closer to it, for teaching and preaching were part of my heritage that I had been trying, unsuccessfully, to ignore.

For some I will always be the voice of 'Thought for the Day' on BBC radio's *Today* programme, while others only know the management guru called Charles Handy whom many assume to be an American, along with most of the other so-called gurus of business. My children, I think, saw me as a benevolent if slightly impractical dad and a fairly decent cook, while my wife had seen me in most of these roles and probably knew better than me the complicated Charles Handy that had resulted and is still evolving. The Charles Handy that I am today only emerged in my sixties, and who knows whether there may not be another version still to come. Call no man happy, or fully himself, until he is dead.

Identity is a puzzling subject. I am constantly shocked by photographs of myself. That is not the person that I see in the mirror each morning, a person who seems more benevolent and, yes, younger than the white-haired old gent in the photos. It is not easy to see ourselves as others see us. Even those dreaded 360-degree appraisals that businesses go in for these days probably reveal only a slanted version of the truth. A friend once described his life as the equivalent of a Wellington chest, one of those small tallboys with some eight drawers. Each drawer, he said, represented a strand of his life, providing a different glimpse of his full self. But it didn't stop there. One drawer was locked to outsiders, while one was locked even to himself – his subconscious.

I was reminded, then, of the old Johari window of my early explorations in social psychology. Created by two professors called Joe and Harry, it consisted of a square box window divided into four quadrants or panes, which you could label A to D, as below:

Known to Others	A	B
	D	C

Known to Oneself

The full window represented your self, as you and others saw you. The idea was that other people looked at you from the side of the window while you saw yourself from the bottom. The divisions between the panes was too thick to see through so nobody saw the whole you. Other people saw the bits of you represented by panes A and D, but not B and C. You saw C and D, but not A or B. In other words, the pane D aspect of you was common to all, but C was yours alone, while B was hidden from all. You would, Joe and Harry suggested, be a better functioning person if you could make pane D as large as possible.

I doubt that this is ever possible. As Shakespeare had it, 'One man in his time plays many parts', but these days he, or she, does it simultaneously as well as sequentially. I am not only different now from the Charles Handy of my youth, I am different from place to place, from one group to another. Are we then the same person or not? Do we confuse ourselves as well as those observing us?

Recently, my wife and I had cause to visit a Delhi call centre. This one dealt with callers to the AOL and Dell helplines from America. Being midday in Delhi it was almost empty because it was still nighttime in the US. The main workforce arrived in the evening. They would then, I was told, change their clothes from Indian to Western, take on an American name, and would, as far as they could, imitate an American accent. They were encouraged to watch American soaps on TV in their spare time and to familiarise themselves with American slang, all so that the callers would find it easier to communicate with them and might believe that they were calling Kansas, not Delhi.

We went away startled at this requirement of a double life. How could they cope, we wondered, being American at night and Indian during the day? No wonder, we said to ourselves, that few stayed more than two or three years even though the pay was good. Then I started to reflect on my own life in businesses and other organisations. I, too, had changed my clothes and my manner when I walked into the offices of the organisation. In some ways I became a different Charles Handy to the one my family knew. We all conform, to a degree, to our surroundings.

Elizabeth, my photographer wife, uses her 'joiner' portraits to illustrate this. She asks her subjects to pose for her in two or three different ways, wearing different clothes or doing different things, to reflect the different roles in their lives, but all in the same setting. In her own self-portrait, taken in her kitchen, she is seen as photographer, as cook, at the stove, and as my agent, sitting behind her computer. She then joins the images together so that it looks as if there are three different people in the room – except that they are all the same person. There is an added twist. Since she takes the portraits from the same position but places her subject around the room, the image that is nearest the camera comes out larger. 'Which of your different personae,' she asks the sitter, 'is most you?' It is often a difficult question to answer. She had no difficulty, though, in her own portrait. Elizabeth the photographer stands proudly in front, with a small Elizabeth hunched over her computer in the background and a slightly larger Elizabeth at the stove preparing the family meal.

What three images of yourself would you choose, I sometimes ask people as they look at these portraits, if Elizabeth were to photograph you? Which would you put up front? Would they change over time and would others agree with your placement? For myself, these days, the most prominent image would be me as an author, holding a book, sitting at my desk or just scratching my head as I figured out what to write. When Elizabeth photographed me a few years ago she used all three of those images. I wasn't too pleased. It suggested that authoring was all there was to me. I wanted to include myself with frying pan in hand, as cook, or, wine bottle in hand, sitting with my family around a laden table. Ten years before I would have included a shot of myself in a business meeting, for those were the days when I wanted to be doer as well as thinker, when I still yearned to be near to some of the people who mattered. Had Elizabeth photographed me in this way every ten years or so it would have been a vivid portrayal of my progress through life, of the different roles that made up the evolving Charles Handy.

When Elizabeth is commissioned by an individual to take a portrait of him or her, she will always ask them to choose their own favourites from the first rough prints. Intriguingly, the choices people make depend on whom they are for. One young woman chose four, each very different from the others. One, she explained, was for her father; in it she had a childlike innocence, quite unlike the one she chose for her mother in which she came across as a competent independent professional, posed beside her computer. Then there was the pose intended for her lover, very tender, very romantic in its appeal and, finally, the one she would keep for herself, the one with a searching quizzical look, serious but touchingly uncertain. She saw herself differently in each relationship. Which was really her? Probably all of them, but few would ever see more than one side of her, and perhaps there were even other possible images that she herself did not know. As the Johari window demonstrates, we are strangers even to ourselves.

Once a year in Britain there is something called 'Take Your Daughter to Work Day' when parents are asked to take their young daughters to work with them to see what the world outside looks and feels like. They also get to see another side of their parent. 'He's a big man there, Mummy,' I heard one daughter say on her return, leaving any implication unsaid. The lion at work is often a pussycat at home, or vice versa. We are often no different from the call-centre workers of Delhi, two people in one.

Does it matter? It can do. One of the big puzzles in ethics is how someone can justify doing things in the business arena that they would not dream of doing in their personal lives, and the confusion that this can cause. Many have found that working with friends or relations is a minefield because the zones overlap. A friend is someone you accept with all their eccentricities and shortcomings as well as their skills and talents. They are who they are, for both good and ill. But that won't do in many a work situation. As their superior or their colleague you may feel it necessary to try to change them, even to ask them to leave.

I was once asked by a friend to help him with his management problems in the charity that he ran. The trustees formally appointed me as a consultant and I spent four weeks interviewing all the senior staff in the organisation. At the end of this period it was quite clear to me that it was my friend, and his aloof and distant style of management, who had created the distrust that pervaded the place and hampered all its doings. I asked him round to a private supper to tell him what I thought, and to suggest some practical things he could do to make things better. He nodded in reluctant agreement and I congratulated myself on a ticklish job well done. My satisfaction was premature. At the trustees' meeting the next week he resigned, after castigating me for sowing discord and making it impossible for him to carry on.

Distraught, we asked him and his wife to supper once again, but he made it clear that he never wanted, as he put it, a touch piously, 'to break bread' with me again.

Since then I resolved never to work for or with friends again, or even to share houses with them. Friendship is too precious to put at risk. The two zones of work and friendship operate best when they don't overlap, because the perceptions of who we are do not become confused. The next problem, however, comes when those with whom you work become your friends. Maybe you outgrow them, or they you. Circumstances can change. The friend and colleague becomes promoted, and is now both boss and friend. Imagine the next appraisal meeting between them. How honest can the new boss afford to be if any criticisms are called for? Should the concerns of the organisation override the sensitivities due to a friend? It would be no surprise if the needs of friendship prevailed and any criticisms or suggestions for change were so diluted that they evaporated in bonhomie.

The truth is that we all behave differently, in a way are different people, in different circumstances. Those who claim that they aren't have probably not stretched those circumstances far enough or seen themselves as others see them. I have often wondered how I would behave under fire in warfare, or in emergencies. Would I rise to the challenge or would I flunk it? Luckily, or perhaps not, I have never been put to the test. All that we can do is to open up that bottom left pane in our personal Johari window as far as we can and perhaps explore some of that top right secret pane, to be open and honest about ourselves instead of pretending to be someone we are not. For many years I lived a sort of a lie, trying to be exactly that, someone I was not – an extravert beer drinker for a time in my youth, a tough oil executive until I was found out, then, later, an aspiring leader of others who, oddly, didn't always seem inclined to follow where I wanted to go. It was a great relief to allow myself to be myself, although I still sometimes wish that I had been born as someone very different. No longer, however, do I try to make that impossible wish become true.

One of the big debates in psychology is whether we have a core identity that is sitting there in our inner self, waiting to be revealed, or whether our true identity only evolves over time. One of the perennial questions that bug organisations is a derivation of that debate – are leaders born or made? The truth, as in most things, is probably a bit of both. The battery of personality tests that purport to show whether we are introvert or extravert, whether we like structured situations or a bit of chaos, are based on the idea that our real identities are formed by early adulthood and that a good life is about finding situations that fit our characteristics. There is some intuitive truth in this. We do grow up, or inherit, some predispositions. One of the more appealing categorisations of these predispositions, by Malcolm Gladwell in *The Tipping Point*, suggests that we are all a mix of what he calls the Maven, the Connector and the Salesman, or, more simplistically, those who are clever and interested in ideas, those who are social and relate well to people, and those who are persuasive and charismatic, with all of us usually more one than the other.

We can't escape our genes, to begin with. I look like my father, with glimpses of my mother. Nice people though they were, no one could call them handsome. Once, when I was due to go to Belfast to address a conference, the secretary there, who was going to meet me at the airport, rang to find out how she might recognise me. Assuming she was talking to my secretary she said, 'I hear he's a round little man.' My wife, for it was she who answered the phone, said, 'Yes, he's actually a round little bald man.' Very like my father in fact. It was a very embarrassed secretary who discovered when she met us that it was my wife she had been talking to. I protested that I was not all that small or all that round, but my wife told me not to be so vain, 'It's who you are that counts, not what you look like.' Maybe, but I have always envied those tall handsome guys with lots of hair and have to keep reminding myself that Julius Caesar was small, round and bald, but still conquered the world and was, by all accounts, thought very sexy by the ladies of Rome.

I am like my father in other ways, too. I think he was always uneasy with power. In his job as a parish priest he preferred the pastoral role, and was a wonderful mentor to young people, showing, one man later told me, a surprising awareness of the trials and temptations, sex in particular, of the world way beyond his country parish. The tough side of running a parish, the decisions, particularly if they had to be unpopular, the need to impose rules and disciplines, the occasional necessity to remove someone for the better good of the whole, these things he found distasteful. I do, too, which is probably why I was never going to be a great manager, of anything.

On the other hand, we do develop as we learn from experience and it does feel as though we are doing more than revealing our inherited selves. We are perpetually filling out our identities, which get firmer and more consistent as we age and begin to discover the spheres of life that fit us best. I think now, on reflection, that I was always mainly a Maven, interested in ideas and knowledge but hankering after more of a Connector's life and wistfully dreaming of being a Salesman. I also discovered, however, both by examining myself and by researching some successful entrepreneurs, that passion can make Salesmen and Connectors out of the most unlikely people. If you care enough you can and will learn to do almost anything. My real trouble was not that I was in the wrong jobs for the first half of my life, but that I didn't feel passionate enough about what I was doing.

Perhaps, too, I was lucky enough to marry someone who, among her many other gifts, is by nature a great Connector and Saleswoman of things she cares about. That can make her partner lazy. Having spent some of her childhood in Austria she also speaks good German, which means that I don't need to learn it. We often de-skill ourselves by relying too much on the skills and talents of our partners, which leaves us incapable and bewildered if they depart.

There are other forms of laziness. One woman described to me how empty her first marriage had been. Indeed, when her husband discovered a couple of years into the marriage that he couldn't have children, his depression and disappointment were such that he didn't speak to her for a year. 'I knew on our honeymoon that it was wrong,' she said.

'So why did you marry him'? I asked.

'I seemed to be on a sort of train at the time,' she told me, 'and I didn't know how to get off. We were abroad and my father back in England had prepared this huge wedding, flaming torches, fireworks, the Bentley, the whole lot. I just went along with it.' In fact she lived with her husband for thirteen years, in a polite façade of a marriage, until she met someone very different who provided the trigger that launched her into a new life and a new and fuller identity, including, now, a daughter. A compromised life can end up as a large chunk of wasted time.

Herminia Ibarra of INSEAD business school interviewed thirty-nine successful people to discover how they had reinvented their lives. They included a literature professor turned stockbroker and an investment banker turned best-selling novelist. She argues that a successful life does not mean knowing what you want to do before you act, but the other way round. Only by acting, experimenting, questioning and acting again do you find out who and what you are. That is certainly my experience. Our identity is partly inherited, partly shaped by early experiences, but it is not fully formed until we have explored more of the possibilities. We should be constantly peeping into that fourth hidden pane and pulling more of it into the daylight. It doesn't make it easy, but maybe by the time we end our lives there will be nothing hidden from ourselves or others.

Life, I now think, is really a search for our own identity. Sad is he or she who dies without knowing who they really are, or of what they are really capable. As we move through life we climb a sort of ladder of identity, gradually proving and discovering ourselves. The psychologist Abe Maslow called it a hierarchy of needs. To me it is more like a ladder. The first rung is that of survival. Can we fly by ourselves, once we leave the nest? Can we earn a living, raise a family, keep a job or get a qualification? Then, survival no longer in doubt, we need to express ourselves, to stand out, in some way, from the others, and so to establish an independent identity. For most of us, success in midlife means reaching this rung on the ladder. But the ladder does not stop there. We still yearn to leave our mark on the world, to make an imprint and to leave it a little different because we lived, for good or ill. The last rung on that ladder, therefore, is that of 'contribution', to something bigger than ourselves, our private bid for immortality, for some lasting memorial. Someone once described Maslow's hierarchy in another way, listing the components of a good life as Living, Learning, Loving and leaving a Legacy. I like that. It captures what I have tried to do in my own life.

The contribution does not have to be earth-shattering. For many, the children that they rear are their best legacy. For others it is the work they do, or the businesses they create, while for some it is the lives they saved or bettered, the kids they taught or the sick they healed, even the garden they made. The sobering thought is that individuals and societies are not, in the end, remembered for how they made their money, but for how they spent it. A headstone that records the millions made by the body buried there impresses none of the passers-by. It is what was done with the millions that counts.

Perhaps it is arrogant even to imagine that the little we can do is of any importance in the great scheme of things. It probably isn't. My books will all be recycled, my ideas forgotten. I know that, but still I write and teach. Why, I wonder? I think that it is because I want to fill up that window, to discover every aspect of myself before I die. This book is itself a part of that search for my full identity. It is a journey through the different Charles Handys who emerged as my life progressed, with the things that I learnt along the way. Do I now know who I am? Not fully, I suspect. There may yet be more to come. In the oft-quoted words of T. S. Eliot, 'The end of all our exploring will be to arrive where we started and to know the place for the first time.' When we cease exploring, however, we might as well die, and I'm not ready for that yet.

Jeff Skoll, one of the two founders of eBay, tells of the day when his father came home with the news that he had been diagnosed with terminal cancer. He wasn't afraid of dying, he told Jeff, then just fourteen years old, but sad that he had not got round to doing all the things he had meant to do in life. In other words, he feared he might die before he had experienced every aspect of his possibilities. Fortunately, in his case, the diagnosis was wrong and he was granted another chance. The rest of us may not be so lucky.

Chapter Two
Irish Beginnings

My postal address for the first twenty years of my life was St Michael's Vicarage, Sallins, Co. Kildare, Eire. For anyone familiar with Ireland in those days, that address on its own would have told them a lot about me. It would have identified me as a Protestant in the South of Ireland, now known as the Republic of Ireland. The vicarage bit indicated that I was a son of the Church, the Church of Ireland in this case, but one linked to (or, as the official wording goes, 'in communion with') the Church of England. That in turn meant that I was one of the Anglo-Irish, not properly Irish and not English either. They used to be called 'the Ascendancy', not a term that was likely to win you popularity among the rest of the population. Anyone knowing that address at that time could have made a reasonable prediction of where I would go to school and college, who my friends would be and which political party I would vote for when I grew up.

Our beginnings do shape our ends, I now realise. And there isn't much you can do about that. As a young boy growing up in the Irish country-side I didn't know anything about my family history or the long and tragic story of Ireland – that came later – but I did know that I was different in some way. I did not know the expressions 'Anglo-Irish' or 'the Ascendancy', but I used to wonder why my mother was so keen that I should not speak with any trace of an Irish accent. We lived in the vicarage, in the midst of the fields, thirty miles west of Dublin, a hundred yards from the beautiful country church where my father said his prayers every morning.

We weren't rich by any means, but we weren't exactly poor. We had a live-in maid and a gardener. They were Catholics and went to Mass in the local village. We went to 'church'. So did everyone else we knew, because they were Protestants and many, like us, the last remnants of the old Anglo-Irish. I suppose that if you are a dwindling minority you cling to any reminder of your identity, even if you no longer believe in it. For most of the Anglo-Irish gentry, the Church was a social not a religious institution; perhaps it always has been. Some of those church-goers still lived in the decaying shells of their once-grand houses and some owned and worked more modest estates or farms, but most were professionals: doctors, teachers, lawyers or architects. I can't remember knowing anyone who might have been called a businessman. That might have been because my parents did not move in the business world, but partly it was because the old Anglo-Irish were not busi-nessmen or women by profession. They were mostly country gentry, many of whose ancestors had come over with Cromwell in the seven-teenth century and had been given large tracts of land in return for their services to the Great Protector who, in Ireland, only protected his own. For many years their descendants ruled Ireland for the English and so came to be known as the Ascendancy.

Some years ago I found the location of the first Irish home of the Handys. It was a ruined castle near Mullingar in the centre of Ireland. We were guided to a pile of stones in the middle of a field by Liam Handy, a very distant relative who still lived nearby and knew the story. The first of the Irish Handys also came to Ireland in Cromwell's wake when he invaded the land with twenty thousand troops determined to exact vengeance for the rebellion of 1641, in which many Protestant planters in Ulster had been slaughtered. Cromwell was not a man given to niceties nor, it seems, were his officers. As Liam told it to us that day, our ancestor had been ordered to capture the castle, which was defended by some thirty Irishmen. Lieutenant Handy offered the defenders safe passage if they laid down their arms. Outnumbered and outgunned, they agreed. When they left the castle he and his men mowed them down. As his reward he was given the castle and its land. No wonder the Anglo-Irish Protestants weren't much loved by their Catholic neighbours, even though some of those Anglo-Irish went on to campaign and fight for the independence of their adopted country.

My mother's family was just one example of the declining grandeur so typical of the Anglo-Irish of the time. Her mother was a Herbert, a distant descendant of the Herberts of Muckross. Muckross House and Estate comprised a large part of the northern shore of the middle lake of Killarney. It was, and still is, a uniquely beautiful site, originally part of the Munster Settlement of 1580 when Elizabeth I parcelled out to her English favourites the land that had once belonged to the Irish Earl of Desmond. The Herberts lived there until 1900 when they sold it to Lord Ardilaun, another of the Anglo-Irish. Legend has it that the Herberts were ruined when Queen Victoria came for a prolonged visit, with all her retinue. Muckross passed through several owners until one of them, Arthur Rose, gave it to the nation in 1932, the year I was born. When I hear the song 'How Can You Buy Killarney?' I always want to reply, 'Just write a cheque.' Sadly, the cheque that was written never came near our part of the family.

We stuck together, we Protestants, for we were a small minority, less than eight per cent of the population then, and much less now. We all went to the same schools and later, if we were bright enough, to Trinity College, Dublin. We banked with the Bank of Ireland, took coffee at Bewley's café, went religiously to the Horse Show at the Royal Dublin Society and hoped to be invited to lunch at the Kildare Street Club – all of them bastions of the old Protestant Ascendancy. Catholic friends were few and far between. There were the Boylans at Millicent House down the road, where Frankie was a friend of my sister and where I played hide and seek in the abandoned attics. There were also the offspring of the really old Anglo families, the Plunketts, Nugents and Brabazons, whose ancestors had refused to follow Henry VIII in turning Protestant but who were as Anglo as the rest of us. I used to meet their sons on the boat going back to school in England on their way to Ampleforth or Downside, the big Catholic public schools. I, naturally, was going to a Protestant school, Bromsgrove in Worcestershire, my parents having reluctantly accepted the advice of the headmaster of my preparatory school that the very few Irish schools for the Protestant gentry would not test me enough. In retrospect the decision of so many of the Anglo-Irish to educate their children in England only emphasised and perpetuated their separation. Many of those children never returned, myself included.

Looking back, I am amazed at the complacency with which we, all of us, including my well-intentioned parents, accepted what was, when I got round to thinking about it, a form of apartheid. Two separate races lived side by side. There was none of the violence that was yet to come in the North of Ireland but the divide was there, partly religious, partly class and all due to history. In his book *Dublin Made Me*, C. S. Andrews looks at the same world from the other side:

> From childhood, I was aware that there were two separate and immiscible kinds of citizens: the Catholics, of whom I was one, and the Protestants, who were as remote and different from us as if they had been blacks and we whites. We were not acquainted with Protestants, but we knew that they were there – a hostile element in the community, vaguely menacing to us . . . they were very respectable . . . their children never mixed with the village children.

I would have agreed, except that I would probably have thought of us as the whites and the Catholics as the blacks. I remember, many years later, coming back from a year in America and asking my mother if anything much had changed in Ireland while I had been away. 'Yes,' she said, 'there have been a lot more mixed marriages.' Still thinking

American, I wondered where all the black people had suddenly come from, then I twigged. She was talking Protestant-Catholic, not white-black. But a cultural apartheid it still was and I had happily lived with it and seen nothing wrong.

Looking back on it all now, I can begin to understand how long-standing tribal differences can bring discord to communities when, to the outsider, they make no sense at all. My parents, and everyone they knew, were decent caring folk, Christian in act as well as belief. They treated everyone they met with courtesy, looked after those who worked for them, believed in equal rights for all. My mother was always ready to help the local Catholic priest when domestic situations required a woman's touch. Nevertheless, we lived in our own tight little Protestant-Anglo world, thought and spoke of us and them, and saw nothing odd about it. How, I now wonder, did I later dare to condemn in my heart those South African friends who lived happily with their own apartheid, being kind and considerate to their servants but isolating themselves from the realities of their country, when I had also lived in a similar, if less damaging, cocoon?

I now realise the force of one's early environment. I can begin to see how easy it is to grow up believing that there is only one way of seeing the world and to accept it without question. That is particularly so if you never meet conflicting views, if you only read the same papers as the rest of your clan – the *Irish Times* in my case – if you go to the same schools, the same parties, join the same clubs and societies. I realise now that you can hold what may seem to be outrageous views on life and society and still be at heart a nice person. I have, belatedly, learnt to look beyond the stereotypes.

The Anglo-Irish have now effectively disappeared, submerged by Ireland's new prosperity. Those country homes are occupied by the new millionaires or have been turned into golf clubs like Millicent House down the road, or Straffan House, where the Bartons lived, which is now the K Club with a course designed by Jack Nicklaus.

Many left, as I did, during the sad period in the fifties and sixties when Ireland seemed to have been left behind by the rest of the world. Unemployment was thirty per cent then, there was no business worth joining and the future clearly lay elsewhere. Get out of the old place as soon as you can was the traditional Irish remedy – and then look back nostalgically to an Ireland that existed only in the imagination. Those of my Protestant clan who remained had no memory of the Ascendancy and saw no point in being anything other than Irish. Indeed, the tradition grew up that the only true Irishman was a Gael and a Catholic, which effectively excluded me. I never went back to work there after my education in England but I carried the memories with me, always.

The religious divide has gone now, too. The change was signalled for me in a dramatic fashion. It was the Christmas after the tragedy of Bloody Sunday in the North, when British paratroopers had opened fire on a Catholic march in Londonderry. My family came over from London to spend Christmas with my parents. The first event was the traditional carol service in the church up the road. 'I think you had better get there early,' my sister said. I looked at her in disbelief. There were never more than forty or so in the congregation even at festivals. 'You'll see,' she said. Indeed, when we arrived the church was almost full. I didn't recognise most of them, but I did notice the young harpist sitting below the altar steps, her fingers on the strings. That was not the sort of thing that my father would normally encourage. Then he entered to start the service. But not alone – beside him was the local Catholic priest. They had decided to have a joint service as their way of saying that the troubles in the North were not to happen here in the South.

Soon nobody was talking of mixed marriages any more. The Catholic hierarchy lifted its ban on attending Trinity College in 1959 and some ninety per cent of its students are now Catholic. Meanwhile the Church of Ireland was withering away with less than one hundred thousand members in 1985 and fewer still today. The Catholic Church, too, had lost a lot of its authority when the paedophile scandals broke. The consumer society had arrived and Ireland was becoming an increasingly secular state.

It was all too late for me, one of the last of the Anglo-Irish. I had left and any opportunity to return had long since vanished. I was destined to be one of those hyphenated figures that are today becoming more common everywhere, people who divide their allegiance between two or more countries and sometimes try to glamorise it as global citizenship. I found it uncomfortable. After our Christmas lunch in the vicarage we would sit down to listen to the Queen's Speech, as most of the Anglo-Irish still did in those days. My mother would defiantly stand up for the British national anthem, which was always played at the end. I could not copy her and was embarrassed by her Anglo enthusiasm, but I was also embarrassed by my inability to remember the words or much of the tune of the Irish anthem.

Which was I, English or Irish? I cherished my Irish passport although I was also entitled to a British one because I was born before 1948. In that year Britain passed the Nationality Act, which finally recognised Ireland's independent nationality and established reciprocal citizenship and trading rights, as well as unrestricted travel between the two countries. The Irish premier responded to this generous act a year later on a visit to Canada by declaring Ireland a republic and leaving the Commonwealth, but my right to a British passport still stands. Even with a British passport I still fail the Norman Tebbit cricket test – I will always support the Irish team rather than the English, even when the odds are against them. Yet to the Irish I am English, in spite of my Irish passport. I once applied to the Irish Department of Foreign Affairs but it was clear that my application was not welcome. I was not a believable representative of my country, despite the fact that my family had lived there for over three hundred years.

Nor was I temperamentally Irish. I am not a gregarious wit, the life and soul of any party or at ease in a pub or bar. I am not even typically Anglo-Irish, a hunting, shooting, fishing countryman. It was a great disappointment to my future father-in-law, who loved his fishing holidays in Ireland, to discover that I did not have a nice estate somewhere over in the West that he could enjoy. I have lived in England for over forty years but I will never feel truly English or even British, although I wouldn't now want to live anywhere else. It was a shock to find, when I was looking for lodgings as a student at Oxford, that many boarding houses had notices on the doors reading 'No Blacks, No Dogs, No Irish'. I can sympathise with the millions of one-time immigrants who are now British citizens but still refuse to be completely assimilated, still wish to assert that one can be faithful to two traditions, the land you came from and the place where you have made your home. In a new land you cling to your roots as a way of keeping your identity. I can feel Irish at heart but still belong physically and emotionally to Britain and, indeed, to Europe. It isn't always easy, but twin or even triple citizenship is both possible and, I believe, desirable if, as seems inevitable, we are going to live and work together as more and more of us go to live and work in lands where we were not born.

Over time I have learnt to rejoice in my role as a member of the great Irish diaspora, the millions around the world who feel Irish in their heart but would never go there for more than a brief holiday. They say that there are forty million in America alone. I discovered, as those Americans have, that everyone has a soft spot for the Irish. Ireland was apparently everyone's second-favourite team in the last football World Cup, after their own. The Economist Intelligence Unit worked out in 2004 that Ireland was the best country to live in for quality of life. Those who lived there weren't so sure, but others envied them.

Ireland is a more ordinary country these days, more like everywhere else. It is the fourth richest country in the world, measured by per capita income. What that means is that the romantic mystique of a tragic history has been replaced by rampant consumerism, rising house prices, traffic jams, pollution, drugs and car thefts. The beautiful coun-tryside of the West is now speckled with a rash of plain white bunga-lows or gabled mansions, each plonked amid the fields with asphalt surrounds in place of gardens. They may be more comfortable than the old Irish thatched cottages that seemed to grow out of the bog, but they certainly lack the charm.

Yes, it is a better place than the embittered, poor, priest-ridden land that I left, a world so vividly described by Frank McCourt in *Angela's Ashes*, but sometimes I think that life was simpler then. We had no electricity until I was thirteen, no heating except for peat fires, no music except the sort we made ourselves. We pumped our own water, grew our own vegetables and collected our own eggs, fetched our milk from the neighbouring farm each morning and cycled everywhere. Each Saturday we lit the boiler so that we could all have baths for Sunday. Other mornings the water had to be heated in a kettle for my father to shave. The rest of us managed with cold. There was a sense of real achievement each evening and a cause for celebration each weekend. No, I wouldn't want to go back to those tough times, but philosoph-ically it was simpler. Life was for living and that was enough.

Now that the physical things of life are so much easier – light and heat at the press of a switch, food from a microwave or a takeaway – we have to find a purpose beyond just living. That's tough. We also have to be good enough at one thing so that we can earn enough to buy all the other things we need. That's tough, too. It pushes you towards selfishness, to care for yourself before you are ready to care for a neighbour. Progress is a funny thing, it is often two steps forward and one backward, or even the other way round.

Not long ago my wife and I were invited to lead a seminar in Dublin entitled 'What Are We Doing to Ourselves?'. The young people who came felt that maybe they were losing as much as they had gained, that some of the good things of the old Ireland – the friendliness, the sense of timelessness, the easy-going life, the family as the centre – had gone with the bad – the poverty, the false religiosity, the island mentality, the sentimentality. Globalisation, they felt, was a mixed blessing. So say many of us, but which nation can sensibly shut its doors to it? Ireland today is a case study of our modern dilemmas, but more than most peoples the Irish are able to talk about them. The Irish haven't yet lost their way with words or their ideals.

Back in 1943 Eamon de Valera, then the head of government, outlined his vision of his country in a speech entitled 'The Ireland that we dreamed of'. One of the most famous broadcasts of the century in that country, it celebrated traditional non-material values. Giving was as important as receiving, de Valera said, service as important as wealth. It was a society in which rights would be balanced with responsibilities, in which adults in their productive years acknowledged non-material obligations both to those who came before and to those who were coming after. The generations were woven together into a seamless social fabric. Sadly, the achievements of de Valera's governments failed to live up to his rhetoric, but the dream lives on. Ireland now has the means to deliver the best parts of that dream, but her will to do so may have been dulled by the seductions of consumerism and the pulling apart of the old communities. Why should one care for one's neighbours, let alone their children, when you may be far away in a few years' time, pursuing an individual goal? It is a problem not unique to Ireland, but, as long as the remnants of de Valera's dream remain, Ireland still has the best chance of resolving it.

Chapter Three
Greek Wisdom

'Just to get us started,' he said, 'I would like you to write me three thousand words on "What is Truth?"' Not exactly a new topic, I said to myself. Pontius Pilate put that question to Jesus as I recalled. He did not get an answer. I don't think he expected one. I was not going to get off so lightly, seeing that it was my Philosophy tutor who was assigning me the task at this, our first meeting. This was Oxford University where I was studying the philosophy and history of Ancient Greece and Rome, having already spent two years translating the classic literature of those civilisations into English and vice versa. What I didn't realise at the time was that my tutor's seemingly straightforward essay topic was introducing me to a very different form of education to the one I had endured thus far. It was only years later that I realised how critical it was to my later life.

It was by an accident of friendship I became a classical scholar. It happened at age twelve when a school friend who needed to learn Greek in order to get into Winchester College asked me to keep him company in his studies. I was happy to agree, little knowing that it was to shape my education for the next ten years. So few people then studied both Greek and Latin that I stood out and was promptly labelled a classicist, ending up studying those languages at Oxford. Beware, I now warn students, of those early labels – they stick to one, whether they are right or not. Who knows – I might have been an enthusiastic scientist. I never got the chance. The Greeks and Romans had me in their grip, whether I liked it or not.

I didn't enjoy the languages much, not being at heart a linguist. When I broke the language barrier, however, and began to delve into the history and philosophy of those two great civilisations, things got better. History I found fascinating. I discovered a growing pleasure in seeking to unravel the causes of things, to reveal the interwoven connectedness of individuals, contexts and events. Historians have always known that life is never as simple as it appears. It was a way of thinking that became part of me. No one told me that I was discovering for myself something that I later found was termed 'systems thinking'. Later on, when I was directing programmes at the London Business School, it was no surprise to find that the best students were often the historians.

Philosophy was another matter. Plato and Aristotle are not easy reading, particularly when there are so many competing attractions during those short Oxford semesters. I struggled, constantly daunted by the tasks set by my Philosophy tutor for the next week's essay. At that first meeting he gave me a selection of readings on truth to help me along, ranging from Plato's *Republic* to A. J. Ayer's *Language, Truth and Logic*. I went away thinking that I had no need of such cribs to write on such a self-evident subject as truth, even if it had baffled Pilate. Later that week I found myself staying up all night, desperately trying to make sense of my realisation that, except in tautologies or some parts of mathematics, there is no such thing as absolute objective truth. It all depends – on the context, the perspective and the starting assumptions. What I call aesthetically beautiful, my wife can see as ugly. It makes for problems when interior decorating is on the agenda. Who is right, which is the truth? Both, I suppose, for I know of no precise definition of beauty. What is obviously true to some is clearly false or mistaken to others. Those who swear in court to tell the truth, the whole truth and nothing but the truth are lying to begin with, because no one can ever know the whole truth of a particular situation. In practice we understand that it is their perception of the truth that we will hear. I have set out to tell the truth in this memoir, but it is only the truth as I recall it. Others, my sisters particularly, often have different memories of the same events. Who is right? Both, or neither. Obvious, once I started to think about it.

For Plato, all that we see or know is but a shadow of the thing itself. It is our perception of the truth, not the actual reality, something that will always remain unknowable. We cannot trust our senses to know what is really there although we have to act as if we do. As David Hume, that pragmatic Scottish philosopher, said, after proving to his own satisfaction that you can know nothing for sure, 'But now I am going to light my pipe and go out for a meal.' And the truth gets even more problematic when we move from the physical world to the realm of ideas. Life, in other words, is one big hypothesis, one, moreover, that is hard to prove or disprove until it has all ended.

For me that first essay was an uncomfortable wake-up call. The world, I could see, was not as simple as I had thought. It might never be what it seemed to be to my eyes. If I wanted to succeed or even survive I would do well to check out the hypotheses that others held about the world as they experienced it to see if they agreed with mine. You can't take truth for granted. It was enough to make one a habitual sceptic, or, more positively, a thoughtful person.

The essay on truth was the first of many. I slowly discovered that the Greek philosophers had anticipated many of our contemporary problems, had even contributed to some of them. Plato took a fairly jaundiced view of the human race. Given most people's selfish and greedy natures, he wanted to entrust his ideal state to a group of guardians, men – always men – reared and educated to take proper care of the interest of the rest. Plato believed in hierarchy. Things worked better when everyone knew his or her place. For her, it was definitely in the home, for him a foreordained role in the state. Below the guardians or the so-called philosopher kings he set the military as the physical guardians of the state, then the business community, the merchants, followed by the free workers, then the slaves. It was a view of the world that infected British attitudes to class and education down the ages. It was, of course, in the interests of the aristocracy to be Platonists. 'Leave it to us,' they would say and believe, 'and all will be for the best for all of us.'

Business, too, was long seen by the British as a lower status occupation, definitely inferior to the armed services. My great-uncle, a crusty old general who first introduced me to a really dry martini, despaired of me when I turned down an invitation to join the British Army in order to work for Shell, accusing me of cowardice. He might have been right, as I privately acknowledged. He even threatened to cut me out of his will. I was dismayed to find, when he died a few months later, that he had done just that. In his view that military service was a worthier occupation than what he called 'trade' he was a thoroughgoing Platonist. He wasn't alone. I was unusual among my Oxford contemporaries in opting for a career in business.

Like Plato, the British reckoned things worked better with a proper hierarchy, one that tended to be fixed at birth. Meritocracy was not a Platonic concept. Democracy was, and is, inefficient, as Plato had witnessed for himself in his native Athens in the later years of its golden century, even if it is less dangerous than the alternatives. I have often thought that it is Plato who gives credibility to the very undemocratic way we run our business organisations, where self-appointed guardians, carefully groomed, determine the way their state is run. I myself was, I later noted, one of those potential guardians at Shell, one of fourteen members of that year's graduate intake, on a special development track and popularly known as 'the Golden Boys'.

Plato's Socrates was the great inquisitor, always questioning, always probing for the underlying assumptions. In later years I remember being told that if you continue to ask 'Why?' three or four times you will eventually get to the bottom of someone's often unconscious motivations. I have used the method myself:

'Why did you adopt this strategy?'
'Because it offered the best return on our investment.'
'Why do you use that criterion?'
'Because that is what our investors expect.'
'Why are they the sole arbiters of your decisions?'
'Because that's the way business is.'
'Why is it that way?'

And so on. Very Socratic and very irritating, no doubt, to be subjected to such an invigilation, as Socrates' unfortunate companions also found. But as a way of teasing out one's basic assumptions and the true reasons for what we do or want to do, it is very effective, so long as it is done politely. When we are in London my wife and I hold open court at breakfast in our home for anyone who may have read our books or heard us speak and would like to test out some ideas on us. We offer no advice but do ask 'Why?' as often as we can. It seems to help people to clarify their ideas. I learnt that from Socrates.

I use the same technique on myself, challenging all my starting assumptions, helped by my wife who knows my prejudices better than I do. It can be an exciting intellectual game, challenging most of the ways things are done in society. The danger, however, is that, like a centipede stuck in a ditch trying to work out which leg moves first, we get paralysed. Sometimes it is best to keep the questions to oneself, as I was to find out soon after I left the safe ivy-clad walls of my Oxford college.

When it came time to decide on a career, I wanted something that took me abroad in comfort, and applied to the great Shell organisation, which I knew spanned the globe. But Shell was an oil company and I was a classical scholar. I apologised at my interview for my choice of subject. 'Don't worry,' I was told, 'you have a well-trained but empty mind, which we will fill with useful knowledge.' Little did Shell know what that earlier training involved. My studies had given me a love of words and argument. I had been taught to look quizzically at conventional wisdom, to question received opinion and to look for alternative approaches to problems. That wasn't a bad training for business, but it didn't go down well with my superiors. The first time I tried it on, suggesting that the oil transportation system in Malaysia could be better organised, the operations director in head office would not even read my report beyond the brief summary.

'How long have you been here, Handy?' he asked.

'Er, six months, sir.'

'And how long do you think this company has been in the oil business in this country?'

'Fifty years?' I guessed.

'Fifty-five, to be precise. And do you think that in six months you know the way things could work better than we do with all our experience?'

'No, sir. Sorry, sir.'

I left the room, still convinced that I was right but calculating that this was not the best time to challenge received wisdom. Events were later to prove me correct, but by that time my report had long since found its way into the sewers of Singapore. I hope that I leant from this episode never to ignore the ideas of the young, no matter how impertinent they may seem.

Partly, I am sure, because of my exposure to Plato's Socrates, I take pleasure today in adopting the contrarian view in a discussion or debate. While this may be useful on occasion, I have come to realise that it may be unhelpful in reaching an agreed decision. Much later in life I did something about it. I decided that my thoughts and advice were best delivered privately, if required, and behind the scenes. After taking the decision I resigned from seven committees or boards on the same day. Only three wrote back to thank me for my contributions – a sign, I sensed, that my departure was not wholly unwelcome, or even noticed.

Plato was difficult, particularly in the original Greek, but Aristotle was almost beyond me. He was Plato's pupil but, I was happy to note, disagreed with him on many points. The trouble for me was that Aristotle knew so much and, in his writings, covered so many fields of human activity, from science to ethics, the arts and politics. He even anticipated Darwin's views on evolution. His ideas have come down to us in the form of his lecture notes and were difficult to understand, for me at least. It is only recently, thanks to a perceptive book, *Creating the Good Life: Applying Aristotle's Wisdom to Find Meaning and Happiness* written by a friend, James O'Toole, that I have come to realise how much Aristotle's views on life had seeped into my consciousness.

It was Aristotle who first introduced me to the idea of 'enough' through his concept of the 'golden mean'. Virtue, he said, was not the polar opposite of evil. It lay in the middle ground between too much and too little. Wealth, to Aristotle, was not necessarily good or bad, as long as it was viewed as the means to something greater. The sin lay in exceeding the mean, the middle point between too much and too little. St Paul may have been right in saying that it was the *love* of money that was the route of all evil, but that did not mean that the rich were necessarily evil – it all depended on what they used their money for.

So what was the 'something greater' for which money might be useful? Here Aristotle has most obviously infected my thinking down the years, even if I had never acknowledged it. To Aristotle *eudaimonia* was what the good life was all about. This complex Greek word is usually translated as 'happiness', but Aristotle means something else. Happiness to Aristotle is not a state but an activity. It is not lying on a beach with a glass of wine and a book, nor having wanton sex with the person of your dreams. *Eudaimonia* is better translated as 'flourishing', or doing your best with what you are best at. Intriguingly, it also applies to organisations, although there our modern business gurus call it 'optimising core competences'. I prefer Aristotle's version.

Aristotle maintained that we are different from other animals because of our reasoning abilities. We alone of all the species are not driven only by our appetites and impulses. Our task in life, therefore, is to make the most of what we start with. Everyone can be successful. Thomas Jefferson understood this very well. His grand declaration of Life, Liberty and the Pursuit of Happiness as the three cornerstones of the American way of life was not a recipe for self-indulgence but a call for all citizens to make the most of their lives.

Immersing myself again in Aristotle after all these years I understand him rather better today and now marvel at how he anticipated so many of our current dilemmas. Life, in many respects, does not seem to have changed that much for us humans down the millennia, despite all the technological advances. But just as his pupil Alexander ignored his wisdom, so did I as a young Oxford student. Maybe there is a time in life for energy, adventure and ambition, and another, later, time for reflection and a sort of wisdom. I regret that I did not take Aristotle or my tutors more seriously when I had the chance. Universities are wasted on the young. There are too many other distractions at that stage in life.

Despite the distractions, however, something did stick from my years at Oxford. Most education is a systematic way of passing on the knowledge possessed by one generation to the next. In that way it acts as a means of socialisation, of accustoming the young to the ways of their elders. Be like us, is the implicit message of our schools and colleges, and you will be all right. It makes for a comfortable world and to some extent it worked when life didn't change that much from one generation to the next. That predictable world is changing, even within one generation. Relying only on what worked yesterday will not help you today; it may even hinder you. Oxford offered you a choice – you could survive by memorising the work of great minds and regurgitating them in the examination halls, but you wouldn't thrive there. It took me a while to understand this and at first I was overwhelmed by a syllabus that required me, apparently, to have read most of the classical texts and the whole of philosophy from early Greece to the present day. I have a bad memory and am easily bored by things that don't interest me. Could I even begin to cope?

I soon found that there was another way. I will always remember, and be grateful for, an early tutorial with my tutor, Reggie Burton. I had translated for him one of Churchill's speeches into Greek prose. He worked his way through my translation, ticking bits and questioning others. He came to a word he hadn't met before. 'I don't know this one,' he said, and opened Liddell and Scott's big Greek dictionary. 'Hmm . . . neither, it seems, do Liddell or Scott. But I think that the Greeks would have understood it and, yes, they would have liked it. Good.' Tick. The book answer doesn't matter if yours is better. That was the message I took away with me that afternoon, and no, I don't now remember what the particular word was.

I still have a bad memory, but it no longer concerns me too much. I now say that a bad memory encourages creativity and I quote the apocryphal Irishman who said, 'How do I know what I think until I hear what I say?'. I learn more by talking and arguing than I do by studying, even though I often surprise myself by what I find myself saying. It took me a while to have the confidence to rely on myself, building on what had gone before but being prepared to leave it behind if need be.

Odd to think, perhaps, that all this could come from studying the Ancient Greeks. But it is not for nothing that my degree, Greats, or *Literae Humaniores* as it was officially called, has long been regarded as the best preparation for those destined to be the guardians in some part of society. It does not matter if, like me, they have forgotten all they knew of Latin and Greek or the details of their history and philosophy, they will have learnt to think for themselves, to express their thoughts cogently and coherently and to apply their reasoning to their own lives. It is, perhaps, what the Shell people meant when they spoke of a well-trained mind, irrespective of its contents.

Many years later, when our son started his stage career, he showed me the short biographical note that he had provided for the back of the programme for his play. I commented that he had made no reference to his education, which had included three years and a good degree at Cambridge. 'Dad,' he said, 'what matters here is what you can do, not how or where you learnt to do it.' The proof of the educational pudding is in the much later eating. Sadly, we don't have many measures of that, only of our exit marks. Oxford prepared me for life in a way I did not recognise at the time. This memoir is, I suppose, a record of what I did with what I was given there. I am grateful, too, that I have now finally got around to Aristotle again. He has helped me to make sense of my later life, to rely less on the approval of others, to refocus my life on *eudaimonia*, and, above all, to cultivate the companionship of my family and friends, another of Aristotle's great themes.

Unfortunately, I didn't know all this back then. Wisdom comes later in life. Meanwhile there were other lessons to learn in the school of life, or in Shell.

Chapter Four
Borneo Lessons

'Do you normally have brandy with your breakfast?'

It was my sales manager, Peter Messum, speaking, looking askance at the glass beside my coffee cup. Peter was my immediate boss. He had come over from Singapore to Kuching in Sarawak where I was the marketing representative for the Shell Company of Singapore, in charge of all the sales of petroleum in Sarawak and Brunei, one half of what was then, in 1959, still British Borneo.

'No of course not, but I've been feeling a bit worn down recently and I find that a drop of this gets me going in the morning.'

This was not true. I wanted out – not from Shell, but from Borneo. I hoped, naively, that my apparent brandy habit might encourage him to look for a replacement. After all, my predecessor had been sent home in a hurry, after being hospitalised with DTs – he'd complained about animals climbing up the walls, the real pink elephant stuff of the alcoholic myth.

I was just twenty-six years old and I had been working for Shell in Singapore, Malaya and Borneo for three years without any home leave. Three years was then the normal contract for an overseas posting, but my time was nearly up and I had an uncomfortable feeling that out of sight might mean out of mind. I was very much on my own in Sarawak with just one other expatriate, Derek von Bethmann Hollweg, who was even younger than myself, to help me manage all our depots and sales outlets in a country larger than England, where rivers were the only thoroughfares and most people still lived in villages in the jungle. There was no telephone connection to Singapore and few people in head office ever felt the need to visit. Borneo was a fascinating land, but Kuching at the end of the fifties was not exactly the hub of civilisation, certainly not for a young bachelor. I was lonely and homesick and dreaming of Christmas in the cold. If I'm totally honest I also wanted to get out before some of my blunders were discovered.

In those days Shell believed in the immersion theory of management development – throw them in and see if they can learn to swim. It has a lot to be said for it, but I would have appreciated just some inkling of the job before I was sent off to do it. I had, after all, been educated in Greek, Latin and Philosophy at university and hardly knew the difference between kerosene and gasoline, let alone the finer points of organising and managing some two hundred people spread over a huge distance. I had been sitting in the regional head office in Singapore pretending to be an economist and trying to forecast the likely demand for oil in South-East Asia when I was summoned to the office of the general manager.

'What do you know of Sarawak?' he asked.

'Not much,' I replied, wondering where this was leading, 'the people are mostly dyaks, Kuching is the capital and they grow pepper.'

'Well, you are going to start finding out a lot more about it. We're sending you there as our marketing representative to take over from our man there who has had to go back to England. You will have to leave before the weekend. It's an exciting opportunity for you, Handy, your first independent command. The sales people will brief you on the market situation. Good Luck!' He rose to his feet with his hand out, my clue that the meeting was over. Before I had time to comprehend what had just happened to my life I was out of the door. That was the Shell that was, as the adverts used to proclaim.

'Exciting' was, I felt, an ominous word, suggesting as many problems as opportunities, as I soon discovered in the offices of the sales department. For one thing, Shell had ninety-five per cent of the market, a number that, I sensed, could only go down. Then there were the airfields where we had one hundred per cent of the refuelling business and there were some six of these spread around this sprawling land of rivers and jungle. Well, I knew how to refuel cars but airplanes were something else again. I had better find out, quickly.

I knocked on the door of the aviation manager.

'I'm taking over in Sarawak,' I told him, 'and I badly need to learn about the aviation business, including the nuts and bolts of the job.'

'Excellent,' he said, his face alight with enthusiasm, 'we'll design a special hands-on course for you, get you putting the stuff into real planes, etc. It'll be fun, you'll enjoy it and learn it all in the best possible way.'

'That would be wonderful,' I said. 'The trouble is I leave the day after tomorrow.'

'In that case,' he looked sorrowful, 'we had better go down to the cathedral and pray.' Which is exactly what we did.

It took two hours in a Dakota to fly to Kuching. I remember looking down as we flew in over the coastline at the endless expanses of jungle and the meandering brown streaks that were the rivers. I looked in vain for roads and discovered later that there were only thirty miles of surfaced roads in the whole country, in and around the few towns. Even the colonial governor's residence could only be reached by water. What sort of world was I coming to, I wondered, and how would I cope? The age-old army principle of 'Carry on Sergeant Major' seemed the only possible answer. Used by inexperienced young officers down the centuries, it might work for me.

I was met by the operations manager, a very competent Eurasian engineer who had, as I soon discovered, been around for quite some time and had seen several young managers come and go. He was to be my eyes, ears and hands-on manager. There was only one problem: he worked by the book and when the problem wasn't covered in the manual he was paralysed. Nor did he think it could be part of his job to improve on the manual or initiate anything. Entrepreneurship was not a word in his vocabulary, and 'experiment' was a word that caused him to shudder. But that was all right – that was where I could come in. After all, I was there to make a difference, wasn't I?

I set out to explore my new territory. To get anywhere in British Borneo in those days, first you had to fly to Sibu, a godforsaken dump then, sixty or so miles up the Rejang, the great river that was the main artery of the country – half a mile wide at Sibu and full of alligators. Then you would embark on a long narrow open boat with a powerful outboard motor on its back driven, you hoped, by someone well versed in this mighty river and its moods. You also hoped that he had keen eyesight because of the logs, which had escaped from the tree-felling operations upriver. They were waterlogged and floated with just the tips showing above the water. Hit one of them at speed and you would be swimming with the alligators. As dusk fell the driver took out his torch to spot the logs while I held my breath and hoped that the next bend would see a landing stage.

The dyaks in the villages lived in their longboats and canoes, and needed petrol to fuel their outboard motors. That was my job – to see that they got it, at the lowest feasible cost. The logistics were silly, it seemed to me. The petrol came up from Kuching in forty-five-gallon drums stacked on the decks of rickety old steamers. Those drums had to be filled at Kuching then manhandled on and off the boats, stored in the villages in highly unsafe conditions, then manhandled back to Kuching again. Costly, inefficient and, most of all, dangerous. So when I met John Reynolds I thought I had the solution, and this time I wasn't going to show it to anyone back in Singapore. I had already learnt that they did not look kindly on new ideas from young upstarts.

John Reynolds was one of those buccaneers who didn't fit into a conventional life. Ruggedly handsome, a great raconteur some fifteen years older than me and an Old Etonian to boot, he had a small bulk steamer and was touting for business. Forget the drums, we thought, put some bulk storage on the village banks and deliver the petrol via his steamer, much cheaper, safer and quicker. But first we would have to do some homework on the possible sites for the five-thou-sand-gallon tanks we proposed. So off we set on a week's recon-naissance of the Rejang villages, chugging up the great river, out of contact with the world for days and nights on end, with just the brown river and the jungle to look at and the occasional alligator for company. There was only one problem – John didn't trust the water, quite rightly, so he turned to sherry instead. We drank it, we cooked with it in a pressure cooker – we did everything except wash in it. Sitting of an evening, tied up by the bank, no sounds except for the jungle noises and the dark water lapping by, John regaled me with unlikely tales of his wanderings, both of us in an alcoholic haze. This was life as I had never dreamed of it. I wondered, just for a moment, what my parents, back home in the vicarage in Ireland, would think if they knew.

Returning eventually to the office in Kuching, I did my sums. The saving on transport costs using John's bulk carrier would pay for the tanks we needed in eighteen months. Singapore was impressed and agreed. The contract with John was signed and the big tanks ordered and installed on the banks of the villages. Four months later John and I set off on our maiden trip. As we passed Sibu some two days out from Kuching and reached the part of the river that I recognised from the times before, something seemed different. The river was notice-ably lower. Yes, said John, it's the dry season and the water level falls considerably. That turned out to be a glorious understatement. When we got to Kapit, the largest of the villages, the new tank was there all right, but sitting some hundred feet above the river instead of where it ought to be, at the water's edge. It was out of reach of our hoses and was dangerously poised way up above us. It was obviously unusable. The same was true in the other villages.

There was no way round it. If we positioned the tanks for the level of the river in the dry season, they would be underwater in the rains. If we catered for the wet season, they would literally be high and dry when the water level fell. I blamed John. He said he was only doing what I asked. It was the sad end to a brief and inebriated friendship. The tanks eventually came back to Sibu where I sold them for scrap – and told no one, ever, until now. And no one noticed, no one in Singapore that is. The villagers did, and the smirks on their faces told me only too clearly what they thought of me.

I didn't need an appraisal interview to tell me how stupid I had been, how I had damaged the image of the company, how gullible I had been to go ahead on my own initiative without taking advice from my staff who had happily, even gleefully I suspect, watched me head for disaster. This was learning by experience if anything was. I was going to have a major task on my hands to restore my credibility. However, if I could fix the mistake before the managers in Singapore twigged, I would have learnt my lesson without the need for further punishment. I decided to make a clean breast of my errors to the staff in Kuching and to ask for their help if they saw me making any further blunders.

Now, as I faced the sales manager over the breakfast table, I wondered if he knew. If he did, he said nothing. Nor, as far as I know, did any of my staff ever mention the affair to anyone. Instead, they gave me a chance to redeem myself, something that doesn't happen too often in organisations, although it should. That was more loyalty and understanding than I deserved.

Later that evening, sitting alone on the verandah listening to the chorus of frogs in the garden competing with Beethoven on the record player, I wondered, not for the first time, what I was doing there. Yes, Borneo had been an interesting, even exciting experience and I was grateful to Shell for leaving me to make my mistakes and correct them unnoticed, but a bit of me knew that this was not the work that I was cut out to do. Others could, quite obviously, do it much better than I. Before he left, my sales manager, wanting to be helpful, commented that I clearly did not take kindly to authority, preferring to do things my own way. 'You will have to rectify that if you want to get ahead in this company,' he said. Ominous words – prophetic, too, as it turned out.

Two months later I was back in London and applying for jobs in business, unknown to Shell. I was still convinced that my future lay in that world, but preferably nearer home. I went for my first interview.

'Have you had any experience of management?' the man asked me.

I drew myself up and, with quiet pride, said, 'Well, I was in charge of a marketing company covering a region the size of England, with some two hundred people working for me, six airports and four depots.'

'Indeed, and where was that?'

'In Borneo in South-East Asia.'

'I see.'

Reading upside down I saw him write 'No relevant experience'.

Not for his purposes, maybe, but definitely for mine. Apart from anything else I had discovered what I didn't want to be doing for the rest of my life. Some might call this negative learning but I saw it as the useful outcome of an experiment. If all your experiments with life work out well then you probably haven't pushed yourself far enough. There may be lives out there that you could have lived had you dared more. When I applied to join Shell I had only the vaguest idea of what was involved or how I would like it or be any good at it. Now I knew.

Borneo was the culmination of my three-year apprenticeship with Shell. It had been an eventful time, all the better, perhaps, for being unplanned. With no formal development programme in place I was available to be slotted into situations as they occurred. This happenstance approach to development had started when I first arrived from the UK in Kuala Lumpur where it was clear that I had not been expected. The young general manager there was not daunted.

'I tell you what,' he said, 'why don't you spend the first two months sitting in my office. Don't speak, just listen and observe. Unless it is very personal and confidential you can sit there all day long or accompany me when I go out on a visit. That will give you a good idea of how the business works and we can set aside some time each evening to talk about what you have observed. Who knows, I might learn as much from you as you from me.' It was the best possible introduction to the world I was entering, even though some of the senior members of staff were taken aback to find me sitting in on their meetings. In time I was entrusted with a series of specific projects to investigate, all under the personal supervision of the general manager. For a new recruit, this upmarket version of 'sitting by Nelly' as a way of learning about a new organisation was both fascinating and invaluable, although two months of silence was quite enough.

One year later, before going to Borneo, in one more piece of happenstance development, I got my first taste of Shell's preference for learning by immersion. I had been summoned to the general manager down in Singapore where the head office for the whole region was located. 'London want us to appoint an economist to cover South-East Asia,' he told me. 'We think you would do it very well.'

'But I don't know any economics,' I protested. 'I studied Greek and Latin at university.'

'But that was Oxford was it not?'

'Yes, it was.'

'Well then,' he smiled, 'that's all right then, you'll cope.' A degree, I suddenly realised, is just a licence to go on learning, the beginning of an education, not the end.

I went out and bought a small yellow book called *Teach Yourself Economics* and read it more intently than any book before or since. The job involved forecasting the demand for oil products in the region. Shell had found that there was a strong correlation between oil consumption and GNP. My problem was that Singapore, still a British colony in those days, had no official GNP numbers. I had to make up my own best estimates if I was to have anything to base my forecasts on. I can't pretend that they were at all accurate and I don't suppose that my forecasts mattered too much in the overall scheme of things, but I can say that if you want to find out what goes on in a country the best way is to try to estimate its GNP. Because I was the Shell economist I had the entrée to a wide range of government officials and businessmen, but I never fathomed the Chinese trading concerns or the likely sales of the wide variety of eating places.

A month later I was asked to address a seminar at Singapore University on the future of the oil industry. I discovered another thing then: if you really want to learn something, try teaching it to someone else. Since by then I knew more than my listeners it should not have been too challenging, but the prospect of the lecture kept me poring over books and statistics far into the night. Ever since I have relished the challenge of speaking or writing for new audiences. I know that I will learn more than they will.

Shell also taught me that people matter most. Soon after I arrived in Singapore I met with Adrian Sharpe, who was then the sales manager. I was, he told me, the first non-technical graduate he had ever had to train. 'What did you study at that university?' he asked.

I repeated my sad refrain, 'Latin and Greek.'

He laughed. 'That won't be much use when you are with the Chinese salesmen whom you'll be managing. I'll take you out to dinner tonight to meet some of them. That will be the start of your real education.' They tried to drink me under the table that night, but at least Oxford had also taught me how to drink. At the end of a long evening it was I who took Adrian home. I had survived the initiation but I began to see that my immediate future would depend more on these folk than on my brains. Ever since I have tried to find out who really makes things happen, often quite low down in the hierarchy, because such people have great negative power. Unless we can trust each other as people, nothing much will get done. In Borneo I also learnt that getting the right people to start with is key to any operation and that first impressions are not always to be relied upon. John Reynolds taught me that.

Later, in my time at the London Business School, I watched one of my colleagues leave to start a restaurant. I met him six months later. 'How's it going?' I asked. 'It must be exciting to be able to apply all your knowledge of effective group working to a real situation.'

'You know what,' he said, 'I have discovered that if you get the right people to start with you don't need all that stuff. And if you don't get the right people it won't be any use anyway.'

Shell had taught me, perhaps unintentionally, that warehoused learning doesn't stick. Unless the lesson and the experience are tied together, the learning evaporates, even if, as in my case, the experience sometimes comes first. That is why, in my view, so much of formal education can be wasted. Shell taught me, in the words of Tom Hunter, the Scottish entrepreneur-cum-philanthropist, that in the world of affairs, 'I Do works better than IQ.' Try saying it out loud.

Experience without reflection, however, doesn't help either. Later I watched my wife as she worked as a volunteer counsellor in marriage guidance. Every counsellor had a tutor whom they met with once a month. Once a fortnight she also met with her group of fellow counsellors to review their casework, under the eyes of a facilitator. The object was not to criticise or blame but to understand, learn and get help. Absolute honesty was required, and the willingness to accept that you had made a mistake or didn't know how to proceed. The appraisal systems that business organisations conduct are what they say they are

– appraisals. Whatever the intentions they are inevitably judgmental and lead to defensive reactions.

Belatedly, some organisations are following the lead of the counsellors. The idea was used by the US Army in the 1991 Gulf War when 'After-Action Reviews' were made part of their programme. These are regular group meetings held after every project or engagement that seek to establish what was the original objective, what actually happened, why it happened as it did, what the members of the group learnt from it and what they now intended to do the next time. I had no group to carry out an AAR but I did the next best thing – I took the trouble to write my own, but privately. Shell in those days did not like mistakes. They wanted a fail-safe system instead of a safe-to-fail culture.

Finally, and most importantly, I unlearnt the main lesson of my earlier schooling, namely that someone else always knew best. I learnt that in most human situations there is no textbook answer, that everyone is different and that you have to make your own judgments most of the time, take your own decisions and then stand by them. Only in technical matters does the expert know better. It was what Oxford had been trying to teach me. In short, I grew up, late, but not too late.

Later on in life, when I found myself in charge of a management programme for up-and-coming executives, I would start off by asking each of the participants to reflect on the most powerful learning experiences of their lives so far. In all the many times I asked that question, I never found anyone who mentioned a course of study in college or later in life. People always came up with accounts of a brush with death, of their own or someone close, of being out of their depth in some situation, or of being stretched beyond their competence. 'So now you know,' I would tell them, 'you will not count this programme as one of your memorable learning opportunities unless it helps you to reflect upon and understand the experiences you have had in the past. If it does it will enable you to deal better with the problems that lie ahead. Experience plus reflection is the learning that lasts.' In my case, I left Borneo, wise as I thought, by then, in the ways of Shell and the world, only to discover that my experiences, and my learning, had only just begun.

Chapter Five
The Golden Seeds

Recently, I was asked to say a few words at the funeral of an old friend. She was Pat Kendall, although when I first met her she was Patricia Rawlings. As I thought about what I was going to say I realised that I had known her longer than I had known my wife. Then it dawned on me that I owed her more than I had realised. She had nudged me through a door in my life at a crucial moment, and I had never thanked her. Finally, I could do so belatedly, if only posthumously.

Pat entered my life in Singapore, when I went there with Shell on my first overseas job. She was one of the splendid women that Shell employed in those days to look after the personal concerns of their expatriates – to help with housing, travel arrangements and all the niggling details that complicate one's life when you change countries. These women often became confidantes, particularly to lonely young bachelors like myself, out of their comfort zone and often out of their depth. I was sad when she departed back to London.

Six years later I headed that way myself. After two three-year spells on the front line in Singapore, Malaya and Borneo it was time, Shell reckoned, for me to return to the centre of things and do a spell at head office in London. The heady days of expatriate living were over. So were my bachelor days. I was engaged to Elizabeth and due to be married in the autumn. I was glad to be going back to London. What I had not expected was the dramatic drop in my standard of living.

When I first met Elizabeth I was the Shell manager in Malacca, on the coast in the southern part of Malaya. I lived in a fine old colonial house with gardens, a tennis court, servants to cook, wash and garden, and an armed guard at the gate at night. There was even a separate villa for guests. Elizabeth's parents came to stay. They were properly impressed by my way of life. That was until they later visited me in London where the home I was offering their daughter was a rented two-room basement flat in South London. 'But you said you had been promoted,' they said, puzzled. I had, but, alas, I was no longer an expatriate, living a kind of fantasy life, I was just an ordinary employee on British rates of pay. Life was suddenly for real.

The promotion was a bit of a disappointment, too. I had a magnificent new title, engraved in metal on my office door – Marketing Coordination Oil, Mediterranean Region. Unfortunately, I also noted that my name was not on the metal but on a plastic slip beneath it. I was clearly what they used to call a 'temporary role occupant'. In practice I was the post office for the Shell operating companies around the Mediterranean. They sent in their requests and I forwarded them to the proper places in the hierarchy, adding comments where appropriate. I had no authority to take any decisions. I was not allowed to visit the countries I was supposed to be servicing, nor to meet their managers when they came to London.

It was, to say the least, boring. For the first and last time in my life I became a clock watcher. The official work day ended, for some reason, at 5.20 p.m. and I left on the dot, only to find that the elevators were always full of other employees also rushing back to their other lives as soon as they were free. It was my first experience of the stress of being underloaded, of too little responsibility. I didn't enjoy my work and, to be honest, I wasn't very good at it. I am sure my shoulders dropped a good two inches every time I entered the Shell building at the start of the day. I spent many an hour just watching the barges going up and down the Thames below my window and noticing how small and insignificant were the figures of the people on the pavement. It wouldn't, I reflected, seem a big deal to get rid of a few hundred of them if one needed to, just a flick of the fingers. Do the directors on the top floors ever let themselves think like this, I wondered?

We often underestimate the problems of role underload. It is as great a cause of stress as the overload that can affect busy people. At least they feel useful and needed, even if exhausted, overwhelmed and at times unable to cope. The underload that I was experiencing was more psychologically distressing. I felt useless and undervalued. The work seemed a waste of my time and of my life. The fact that I stuck with it because of the money they were paying me only made me feel some sort of accomplice, as guilty as the rest of them. I wanted to hit back at the organisation in some way. It was then that I realised that I might not have any authority to do anything positive in my job, but I did have negative power. I could stop things.

One day the mail brought me a capital investment proposal from our Italian company. They wanted to build a refinery in the Bay of Naples. My job was to forward it to the proper committee. This time I didn't. I binned it instead. A refinery in the Bay of Naples would be aesthetically wrong, I felt. In time, of course, the Italian company realised that their proposal had gone missing and sent another, this time copying it to all and sundry. They got their refinery but I had, at least, delayed it for a while. I am not proud of what I did that day but it helps me to understand why other frustrated workers can be tempted to activate the negative power that even the most humble possess. The girl in the call centre who puts the phone down on me, the waiter who ignores me, the official who refuses me planning permission for no obvious reason, the airline staff who close the gate just as they see me rushing up – they may all be exercising their negative power because it was the only way they had of demonstrating that they mattered. In one recent British survey, seventy-two per cent of workers said that they were dissatisfied with their organisation. Nineteen per cent wanted actively to sabotage it. Looking back to those days in the Shell head office, I know how they feel.

Then, one day, my boss put his head around the door.

'Could you come to my office for a moment?'

'Of course.' What could he want? We didn't communicate much. I thought he was wasting my time and my brain. He thought I was inadequate for the job and a waste of his resources. He might even have been right.

'I have had this rather odd request,' he said. 'The powers that be want me to release you to be the assistant manager at the management training centre at Shell Lodge.' He clearly thought that those powers had lost their reason. 'It's a pity because you were just beginning to get the hang of this job, but I have no good reason to keep you, so I have agreed to release you.'

Shell Lodge was a Victorian mansion set amid spreading lawns on the banks of the Thames near Kingston. It is now a housing estate, but back in 1963 it was a glorious country estate in the suburbs. There was even a four-bedroom house that went with my job. Shell Lodge was used to house the senior and middle management training courses, some eighteen people who stayed there for six to eight weeks. My task was to manage the middle-management courses, the equivalent of the staff-college courses run by the army, a necessary rite of passage for those thought to be heading upwards in the organisation. The design of the programmes was in the hands of the personnel department in London, but I had to make it happen. I couldn't believe my luck.

It was only when I met my new boss and his wife in the Lodge that I realised what had happened. He was 'Weary' Kendall, a wonderful Shell veteran whose nickname had stuck – I never did know his real first name. And he was now married to the person I knew as Pat Rawlings. Pat, I recalled, was a close personal friend of Shell's head of personnel at the time and had, I assumed, wanted one of her old charges back in her care. Perhaps she had even heard of my unhappiness and still saw herself as my benevolent guardian in the big impersonal corporation.

The job was used by Shell as preparation for the next overseas posting. It was not part of their plan that I should be seduced by the task. I found, however, that I was fascinated by the educational challenge of preparing these young managers for the wider world they were due to face. I knew, instinctively, that I had found my calling. So when Shell came up with the next job, that of manager of their company in Liberia, I told them that I didn't want it. I wanted more of what I was doing. That was not on offer. So, without knowing what I would do instead, I sat down and wrote my first ever letter of resignation.

It seems a simple thing, as I write it now, but in those days people did not leave Shell, particularly if they had no alternatives arranged. For the first time in my life I was not in the care of an institution. I was on my own and, yes, it was scary. But, unknown to me, Pat and my wife were plotting. Seeing the way my mind was working, they got in touch with 'Sinbad' Sinclair, who had been the London regional manager for South-East Asia when I was out there and was yet another old chum of Pat. As my good luck would have it, he had retired from Shell and was then chairing the Foundation for Management Education, a body set up by business leaders to found and fund the first graduate business schools in Britain. He recommended me to Dr. Arthur Earl, the designated principal of what was to become the London Business School but which was, at the time, just an office with a filing cabinet and a telephone.

'What can you teach?' Arthur Earl asked me.

'Well, Management, I suppose. That's what I have been doing.'

'We won't be teaching Management,' he said, to my astonishment, as I began to wonder if I had come to the right place. He went on, 'We will teach Finance, Marketing, Economics – the elements of management. Can you do any of those?' I told him that, unfortunately, I was not qualified in any of those areas – I had (the old apology once again) read Latin, Greek and Philosophy at university.

'Good,' he said, 'then you can teach Logic. Managers badly need logic. But you could also run a prestige programme that we hope to get money for from the Sloan Foundation – it is a mid-career sabbatical programme for selected executives.'

So my future was decided, in the way these things often are, through a mixture of timing and good connections – and Pat. It is only now, looking back, that I can properly appreciate her contribution, how she rescued me from the torture of head office and eased me into a life for which I was much more suited, once she saw where I wanted to go. She never talked about it, never offered advice, never presumed to know me better than I knew myself, just acted when she thought it might help and never, ever, referred to her part in it, which, I suppose is why I never got round to thanking her.

She had one more little nudge to give me, although I didn't understand it at the time. At the private farewell party that she and Weary gave us, Pat produced a parting gift. I unwrapped the odd-shaped parcel, intrigued by its possible contents. When it was finally free of its packaging I was, for a moment, lost for words. It was a non-stick frying pan, a new innovation in 1965, Teflon being one of the first by-products of the American space programme, but it was not quite what I had been expecting. Maybe she was just giving us something useful in our new life, but, looking back on it, the thought occurs that she was gently suggesting that there might be other things in my life than work, that a man's role conceivably might extend to the kitchen. If so, she was, once again, anticipating what was to become a significant part of my future.

At a recent conference the lecturer invited us to list the three or four people who had had the most influence on our early lives.

Teachers figured prominently in the lists, as did mothers, although seldom fathers, I was sad to note. At the top of my own list I had to place Elizabeth, my wife, whose unfailing belief in my abilities is daunting and challenging but I followed the others in listing two teachers, Sam Darby, the Classics master at Bromsgrove, who had enough confidence in me to put me forward for an Oxford scholarship, and Jim Ball, the principal of the London Business School, who rashly appointed me a full professor before I had the proper credentials, published papers and serious books. It can be frightening to find that people have such faith in your potential – you have to live up to it. And now there was Pat. Ruefully, I realised that I had never thanked any of them properly. When Elizabeth and I wrote a book about the people we called the 'New Alchemists', entrepreneurs of one sort or another, a striking feature of their lives was the intervention of some respected figure in their early lives who had given them the self-belief and confidence to set out on their own. I discovered after writing the book that Freud had called this a 'golden seed'.

Often the seed was just a chance remark, but it could be the loan or gift of money at a crucial time, a critical introduction or recommendation or the chance to take on unproven responsibilities – all hard evidence of someone's belief in your abilities. When Dee's teacher told one of our Alchemists, almost in passing, that she had got the best grades in the region in her examinations, she never forgot. The seed had been planted. Later, when she applied to a medical school she knew she would succeed even though she was over the recommended age because, 'You see, I knew I was clever.' I wonder if Dee ever thanked him.

I know now, from my own experience, that teachers, parents, partners, even managers, have to live vicariously. That is, they have to take private satisfaction from the public achievements of those they have nurtured, taught or directed, because those who have benefited seldom realise it at the time, or, if they do, take it for granted as only their due. If one is lucky, they do come back when enough time has passed.

Acknowledged or not, the planting of golden seeds, by deed or word, is one of the most pleasing and perhaps important things that anyone can do for someone else. The world is short of such seeds. Sometimes it seems culturally inappropriate, as when an old-school business leader growled at me, 'They don't need me to spell it out, they know they're doing OK unless I yell at them.' The golden seeds seldom get sown in a formal appraisal setting, probably because some positive comments are part of the required ritual of such occasions. Nor do seeds casually thrown around like confetti ever germinate, because they aren't meant or taken seriously. They have to be genuine and sincere, and can even be anonymous. I once received a card from someone I had never heard of. It just said 'I read your last book. Thank you.' It had no return address, I could not reply. That spelt sincerity for me. It was heart-warming and encouraging, for writing is a lonely job.

Pat Kendall knew nothing of golden seeds, but her belief in me and her desire to help where she could was a great boost to my morale as I struggled to start a new life. What I had not expected was that the prelude to that life would be in America. It was going to be at least a year after my meeting with the new principal of the London Business School before the funding from the Sloan Foundation was confirmed. It seemed sensible for me to learn how the two American Sloan programmes worked, and MIT had offered to host me for a year while I studied their experience. The Foundation for Management Education, 'Sinbad' Sinclair again, were offering grants to those who wanted to apprentice themselves to business schools in America, given that there were no university business schools in Britain at the time. So it was that with a six-week-old baby girl we flew to Boston in May 1966. America was still an undiscovered country for most Europeans at that time, much discussed, but seldom visited. Kennedy was dead, the Vietnam War was under way, the civil rights marches were headline news and American prosperity was something to be envied by a still impoverished Britain. We tingled with anticipation.

Our arrival at Logan Airport in Boston gave us a taste of our new country. It was a hot and humid afternoon and the immigration officer was not in a happy mood. He bulged out of his sweat-stained shirt and frowned at us.

'You come from a smallpox area, where are your vaccination certificates?'

We had expected this because there had been a case of smallpox in a Southern German city a couple of months back. Our certificates were up to date, except for our baby. Our doctor had advised against vaccinating someone so young and had given us a letter to that effect. This carried no weight with our officer.

'We will have to put you all into quarantine for four weeks,' he said, and disappeared into a back office to make arrangements, while we looked at each other in dismay.

When he returned I explained that my appointment started in three days. I had to be there. Nor could I afford to pay for hospital bills for four weeks. My wife pleaded. He began to sympathise with our plight. If I would commit MIT to an indemnity of seven million dollars should it turn out that we were infectious, he would let us through. He produced a typed document. I signed it on behalf of MIT, which, of course, I had no right to do.

As we went to collect our baggage I reflected that this was indeed a new country. I liked it. Here was a man who had used his initiative to get around the rules in order to help a couple in some distress. He knew that I had no authority to sign on behalf of MIT, but he had his piece of paper that he could show to any who asked, should he ever need to. He had trusted us, had found a way round, had compromised and done it all without having to get permission from any superior.

Some years later we were travelling in California. When we reached our hotel in Los Angeles we realised that we had left our passports in the safe in our room in San Francisco. We rang the hotel. They put us through to the maid who had serviced our room. She looked in the safe and found our passports. 'I tell you what I'll do,' she said, 'I will give them to Federal Express, marked Express, and they should be there in the morning. No don't worry, the cost is on us.' Great service, and a great organisation to have given her so much authority.

Gumption. That's what I liked, and the willingness to help. There was an energy there that I had missed back in Britain at the time, and an infectious enthusiasm allied to a boundless confidence. I agreed with Isaiah Berlin who once described Americans as 'an open, vigorous, 2 x 2 = 4 sort of people'. Anything then seemed possible. Vietnam was still winnable, maybe. The moon landings were in sight. At a supper party soon after we arrived we were brainstorming new business ideas. In Britain this would have been a fun party game but this was America. The next morning I got a call – 'Great idea, that one of yours, Chuck, I've had a word with my banker and I can get the collateral – so when do we start?' And no, we didn't do it. I didn't like the 'Chuck' instead of Charles, and I didn't like the risk. I was still too British.

Most of all I appreciated the way my background fell away from me. In Britain as soon as I walked into a room and opened my mouth people would have a reasonable idea of what sort of family and background I came from. Not so in America. They could tell I was British because of my voice, even when I protested that I was really Irish, but beyond that they could not place me, nor did they want to. They took me as they found me. It was the sort of freedom from one's past that I imagine many immigrants also rejoiced in.

Alexis de Tocqueville was my tutor on things American, his

comments still as valid, it seemed to me, as they were when he went there in 1831. He remarked on the absence of a land-based aristocracy and the independent spirit that was the result. He also commented that he knew of no country 'where the love of money has taken stronger hold on the affections of men'. I, too, was intrigued and, I must admit, slightly shocked, by the way money seemed to be the measure of most things, particularly in my business school. Americans claim to want both liberty and equality but seem quite prepared to trade economic equality for individual liberty, with the result that they have the most economically unequal society in the developed world. Yet, strangely, there is no serious socialist party to rectify this. I came to the conclusion that it must be the power of the American dream, the belief that everyone can make it to the top through their own endeavours, that reconciled the poor to their state. Individual liberty also implied individual responsibility for one's own destiny.

After my institutionalised life in Britain, where I had never been without the protection and the guidance of an organisation of some sort, this was an eye-opening tonic, particularly in my new unprotected state. I was beginning to understand that my future life would depend almost entirely on my own efforts. My year in America, I could see, was going to be an invaluable preparation, as much culturally as intellectually.

Actually, I discovered, that culture was partly our, British, fault. The American culture owes a lot to the Puritans, who fled from Britain to their new-found land. The Puritans lived in expectation of something new, even the restoration of Christ's reign on earth, which they, his living saints, were responsible for bringing about. The Puritans also believed that being well off through your own efforts was a sign of God's approval. There was nothing wrong with outward signs of wealth and status as long as the pleasure they gave was neither profane nor licentious. Because money earned is money to be proud of, it becomes the easiest way to reward effort and creativity as well as the simplest way to give something back to society. Philanthropy, then, is the polite way of advertising a life well spent.

There was much in this that was strange to me. Winston Churchill once said that if we wanted a wealthy society we would have to tolerate wealthy men. In America they didn't tolerate them, they admired them, provided always that the wealth had been decently earned. They were paraded in front of us at MIT's Sloan School of Management as heroes to emulate and they gave generously to the school to enable it to produce more such as them.

Brought up to think of money as something necessary but slightly distasteful in excess, I found this strange. I came to see, however, that it is not money in itself that needs to be looked at askance, but the use to which it is put. In certain walks of life, particularly business, money is the outward measure of success. If those who have earned it then use part of it for the benefit of society, everyone wins. In America philanthropy is not charity but a way of investing for a better society. In Britain we used to think that the future of society was the job of government. If we paid our taxes that should be enough contribution. It was an attitude that fuelled the perception of business as a selfish occupation.

Things are slowly changing in Britain. The great bulk of the adult population does some voluntary work. The new rich are more American in their willingness to be seen to be giving back to society, with their money but, as valuably, with their time and experience. The best philanthropy may be anonymous, but if a culture of giving back is to grow, some people need to stand out as exemplars. Business itself is beginning to see that part of what has been called its 'licence to operate' in society should be a visible contribution over and above the taxes it pays. To dismiss this new sense of responsibility as just good public relations is unfair.

In 1967 I wasn't sure that I would be able to create the same atmosphere back in London. Instead, I carried back from America that other message, that the future is ours to create, that everything is possible if you care enough, that people should be allowed and encouraged to use their initiative. For many years thereafter I went to America for an annual injection of energy and optimism. My year in America changed my attitude to life.

Chapter Six
Schools for Business

There were once three occupations in Britain for which you required no qualification and for which no training existed: politician, parent and manager. Unfortunately, they were also three of the most important. Management, in particular, was something that, it was felt, everyone could do at a pinch. Rather like making love, it was something that sensible people instinctively knew how to do, when and as the need arose.

But then, as I discovered, even lovemaking isn't quite as natural as people assumed. Nowadays there is such an abundance of explicit magazines, films and books demonstrating just what goes where and how that no one can be ignorant of how it should be done, even if not always expert in the execution. I had only a strange magazine called *Health and Efficiency*, a nudist publication, to acquaint me with some rather bowdlerised photographs of the female body – even James Joyce's *Ulysses* was banned in the Ireland of my youth. I learnt by experience in due course, but not without much fumbling frustration and gaucherie.

Parenting wasn't much better, although my young wife and I did have Dr. Spock's bible *Baby and Child Care* at our side, by day and night. Then there were always mothers and mothers-in-law all too eager to advise. Looking back, I can only apologise to our two children. Our daughter once, half jokingly, accused us of using her as a social experiment in her education. She did not know the half of it. All her early life was an experiment, as it inevitably is for the first child of first-time parents.

Management didn't even have a Dr. Spock. There was no decent book, as far as I can recall, back in the fifties in Britain, to which a would-be manager could go for help. The first remotely readable book, *The Human Side of Enterprise*, by Douglas McGregor, a professor at MIT, was not published until 1960. Shell was very taken by McGregor's book, in which he distinguished two styles of leadership. One, Theory X, worked on the assumption that people needed to be told what to do, while Theory Y assumed that people could be trusted to act responsibly on their own initiative. Shell memorably sent out a circular to every manager in that year, summarising the book and decreeing that, with immediate effect, Shell would be a Theory Y organisation, unaware, presumably, of the confusion they caused by using Theory X to implement Theory Y. Old habits die hard.

The thought of actually going back to school to learn about management struck people as bizarre, or so it certainly seemed to both Oxford and Cambridge universities who each turned down the invitation from the business community to establish graduate business schools along American lines. 'We are not a trade school,' one professor said, indignantly. That was in the early sixties when the government in Britain, urged on by a group of leading business people, had begun to worry about the state of British management and how it might be better educated. It was right to be concerned. Thirty years later, as part of 'The Making of Managers', a 1987 report for the government that I chaired, I calculated that almost every business executive at that time would have left school at fifteen and not had one day of formal education since. This was because only eight per cent of school leavers in those days went on to university and they almost all went into the professions or the civil or colonial services. Business had to make do with the 'University of Life', as the managers of the day defiantly termed it.

There were two exceptions: the alumni of the armed services and accountants. The armed services took management seriously. They trained their officers on recruitment and, later, at their staff colleges, where mid-career courses for high flyers lasting up to a year were the norm. Many British managers in the fifties and sixties had done their national service and had been exposed to the management theories and practices of the armed services. They carried this experience into their new business careers and, for a time, the businesses of Britain bristled with the equivalent of officers' messes, where the managers enjoyed three-course luncheons while the lower orders made do with the works canteen. It often took time for the new ex-servicemen to understand that business organisations operated in a different world, one where the right to command had to be earned and where they could no longer count on the ready acceptance of authority and the privileges that went with it. No one ever suggested that training to fight a war was the right preparation for managing a business. It just happened to turn out that way, the unintended consequence of the national need for military preparedness.

The best preparation, however, for a management role in business was generally thought to be an accountancy qualification. In preparing my report 'The Making of Managers', I unearthed the intriguing fact that Britain had 168,000 qualified accountants compared with four thousand in West Germany, six thousand in Japan and twenty thousand in France. We didn't need or use that many accountants. The great majority were not working as accountants at all, but as non-financial managers in business organisations. There is nothing wrong with the accountancy training – for accountants. But accountants are taught to give priority to the visible financial costs and assets, not to the less quantifiable human assets, which they regard as costs. They focus on the past rather than the future, because that alone can be accurately measured and audited. Their training regards risk, uncertainty and the unknown as undesirable. People management, at that

59

time, had no place in the curriculum, for money and its measurement was all that mattered. The accountancy professions had, accidentally, become the business schools of Britain. No wonder our economy was lagging behind that of our competitors.

I didn't know all that back in 1965 as I prepared to leave Shell. I was just hugely excited by the discovery that there were such things as places in universities where one could learn all the secrets of business and organisations and how to run them. A few of my generation had known of the Harvard Business School and its competitors, had even won Harkness fellowships to study there for an MBA, a degree that was unknown to me. But I had been immersed in South-East Asia, where such things were not talked of. Little did I know, back then, that I would be privileged to study at one of the leading American schools, would help to build one of Britain's first two graduate schools, would later play a leading role in the first course of what was to become the Open Business School of Britain's Open University, would act as advisor to Cambridge University when it belatedly got round to establishing its own business school and would chair the 'Making of Managers' task force that helped to fuel the blossoming of management education in British universities in the nineties. In the process I learnt a lot, about management, about education and about the learning process. I now believe that we and I got a lot of it wrong, but, as in much of life, if we had waited for perfection we might never have got started. Looking back now, after forty years, I can see that, if nothing else, we helped to make the study of management and business respectable. So much so that Business Studies is now the most popular undergraduate course at most British universities. Given the anti-business culture of the land when I left for America, that must count as a cultural revolution. It was exciting to be a part of it.

I was full of excitement and trepidation when I arrived at the Sloan School of Management at MIT one sunny May day in 1966, having survived the immigration process. So ignorant were we in Britain, at that time, of things American and of business schools that one of my friends, hearing that I was going to study what he called Commerce at MIT, thought it must be the Montreal Institute of Typing that I was headed for. I knew, however, that the Sloan School was one of the top ten business schools in the world, that MIT was famed for its engineering and science schools and that it had one of only two sabbatical year programmes for high potential managers in mid-career, the other being at Stanford University Business School in California. The director of the MIT programme, one Peter Gil, sensibly suggested that the best way for me to get to know the programme would be to participate as a normal student. Thus it was that I joined fifty large crew-cut American male executives – no women then – for a year of full-time management study.

I remember thinking that there must be, in the Sloan Library, the secrets of good management, that the scholars and researchers there must long ago have found out what worked and what didn't and that all would soon be revealed to me. I felt that I had been deprived, during my ten years in Shell, of all the accumulated wisdom that must lie on those shelves. After all, if there were such a thing as Management Science, presumably there would be scientific laws and rules. I was to be grievously disappointed. I read endless hypotheses that tried to explain why people and organisations behaved as they did, but no proofs. I ploughed through secular sermons, case histories and books of tips, but remained confused rather than enlightened. Managing a business, or any organisation, I came to see, was more practical art than applied science. Yes, there were some useful disciplines, as in any art form, but what worked best could not be wholly determined in advance. Every situation was different. The actors, the motives, the resources, the constraints were never the same.

The discovery came, unexpectedly, as a great relief. It meant that ingenuity, imagination and character still had an important part to play. The world of organisations was not firm and fixed like a piece of engineering. An organisation was more like a mini society, one in which anything could change or be changed. Not that that inhibited the teachers of the Sloan School from trying to reduce the management process to teachable formulae. It was my first blinding insight – that schools, at every level, prefer to teach what can be taught, rather than what needs to be learnt. It was to colour all my future thinking about education.

Economics was a staple subject of our first semester. I was not expecting to be troubled by the subject. I had educated myself in economics at Shell and had worked as a business economist for a time, both for Shell and in the interval between leaving Shell and going to America. That was until we took the examination at the end of the semester. It was a multiple choice examination paper, which, the professor irritatingly informed us, had been marked by his ten-year-old son, who had only to check our ticked boxes against the crib. I scored twenty-three out of one hundred, the lowest in the class. I was shocked. The problem was that I had ticked the box 'none of the above' in too many instances, believing, as I saw it, that the correct answer often depended on the circumstances. In time I learnt to play their game, if only to ensure that I got the degree, but I disliked the over-simplification and reductionism that was involved. It was only later that I myself came to see that you have to oversimplify things some-times in order to begin to understand them. Only when the basic frameworks are established can you add in the qualifications and complexities. Perhaps, I now think, it was injured pride rather than undue simplification that triggered my annoyance.

The basic rules, as the professors defined them, were complemented by case studies, in which we were presented with piles of data about a business situation and were required to discuss what we saw as the problem and what to do about it. These were useful exercises in analysis, in sorting out the wheat from the chaff in the accumulation of infor-mation and in trying to formulate a way forward. It was, for me, a new and exciting way to study, with real problems as the meat rather than pages of a textbook. My worry, however, was that the case studies inevitably passed over one of the main problems of real life, the actual collection of the data, including, particularly, the assessment of the individuals involved. The case-study classes also suggested, by implication, that the analysis was key and that implementing the decision was secondary. Too often, however, I have found that knowing what one ought to do in a situation is easy; it is the doing part that is tough. But that, of course, could not be tried out in the classroom, so it, too, was seldom discussed. Fascinating though these classes were, I worried, with my future role in mind, that it all made management look easier than it really was.

I enjoyed my time at business school. It was fun to be learning again. It was pure self-indulgence to have a whole year in which to invest in myself, to have no responsibilities to anyone except myself and my family. If I failed I let myself down, not the organisation. I did not need to worry about budgets, about whether my staff was happy or the customers content. I had none of either and it was bliss. But did I learn anything useful there, I ask myself? My answer is simple, but a little paradoxical. I learnt something very important – that I need not have gone. By the end of my programme I realised that I had really known most of the important things all along. But I had to have gone there to find that out. By that I don't mean to diminish the experience. We all go through life accumulating a bundle of private learning. Much of the time, however, we don't know that we have it. It is lodged in our subconscious. To make it more readily available when we need it we have to drag it out into our conscious mind. That was what MIT did for me. It is what most people get from what are, rather oddly, called post-experience programmes.

To find out that you know what you didn't think you knew is not trivial. You leave feeling that you can now tackle most of the problems of the organisation – if those at the top will let you. Nor were the more technical parts of the programme irrelevant. Just to know that such things as discounted cash flow existed and how it could be used was a boon. I could now, I felt, talk in a moderately intelligent fashion to the accountants and the consultants that always seemed to hover around organisations those days. Management, I had discovered, is not something mysterious or conceptually difficult. Its difficulty lies in applying the ideas, not in the ideas themselves. That realisation was a huge boost to my self-confidence and worth all the time and effort. It was to be another key to my theories about education. It is, in the end, aimed at giving someone the self-belief that enables them to take charge of their own life.

That is not to dismiss the particular skills and knowledge that help us to access and apply the deeper learning that can enrich our personalities and our lives, but these are no substitute for what I was beginning to see was the real thing, realising what we already knew, privately and subconsciously, and understanding it. Only then can we use our knowledge effectively. Experience and learning have to go hand in hand, and in the same time frame. Providing the concepts before the experience is to store learning in a mental warehouse in the hope that it will come in useful later on. In my experience, however, warehoused learning decays very rapidly. Too often it is no longer there when you come to need it. We know that to learn a language you have to use it as soon as you can after you learn it. It is no different with everything else.

I relished America and was seduced by its ways. I returned to London determined to help build a modified American-style business school in London. I was resolved that the programme that I would be directing would put more emphasis on helping the participants to make sense of their own past experiences, would take them outside the classroom more and would encourage them to think for themselves rather than take the teaching of the faculty for granted. My new colleagues had already got started and, alumni one and all of American business schools, they, too, were eager to apply parts of the American model to poor benighted Britain. We had the confidence, or perhaps the arrogance, of youth. Our average age must have been around thirty-five and we felt it our mission to change the way in which business was done in Britain. We would take the best of American experience and adapt it for a better Britain. It was a heady time.

Why, I now wonder, did we not pause to consider how we, in Britain, organised the training and development of our other professions before adopting without question the American model? Professional accountancy courses may have been inappropriate for learning about management, but the way they and their kindred professions of law, medicine and architecture had been educating their future professionals did seem to have stood the test of time. They all consistently mixed formal learning with some form of apprenticeship. Not only did this combine theory and practice in the way I had felt was essential, but the hands-on apprenticeship model allowed their pupils to earn while they learnt. Useful. It is the same mix of classroom and workplace that the French call 'formation' that is at the heart of their *grande école* system. We, following the Americans, were locking our students into classrooms for two years and charging them a huge fee for the privilege. To pay off their debts they naturally looked for their subsequent employment to the lucrative areas of consultancy and banking, fields for which, as it happened, they were well prepared by the stream of case studies that had been their diet for two years, allied to the skills of analysis and measurement. The MBA degree, or Master of Business Administration, the old word for management, should really, I felt, stand for Master of Business Analysis and that, as it happened, was exactly what the consultancy and banking firms wanted.

The trouble, as many more normal businesses were quick to point out, was that this learning did not equip the new graduates for practical management, nor were the firms prepared to pay these untried apprentices the sort of salaries they could earn in the banks and consultancies. Thus it was that, with few exceptions, the great bulk of Britain's business world was going to be left untouched by our efforts.

My own way round this dilemma was devious. I set out to select for the programme only those who, as I put it, did not need to come. As I saw it, there were aspects of management that we might talk about in the classroom but could not develop there. They included, principally, relationship skills – the ability to work with people, to persuade them, excite them and, where necessary, discipline them. They would also need imagination, perseverance, courage, a degree of self-knowledge and an ethical stance in life. Nowadays many of these qualities are encapsulated in the concept of emotional intelligence, but that phrase had not been invented then. If they possessed these attributes, I argued, then we could add some useful skills, principally of analysis, that would make them even more effective as managers. But if the preconditions were lacking then analysis alone would not help.

In practice, I believe, most graduate business schools do as I did, although they conceal their reasons by making what they call 'relevant experience' a precondition of entry. Even then, however, the classroom learning was too far separated from any opportunity to test it out in the arenas where it would later be needed. The result was often to leave the students with a distorted and narrow view of their responsibilities. Harold Leavitt, a distinguished professor of Stanford Business School, goes further, saying, 'We have built a weird, almost unimaginable design for [business] education that distorts those subjected to it into critters with lopsided brains, icy hearts and shrunken souls.'

In 1981 Britain's Open University allocated a small sum of money for a pilot course on management. It was called 'The Effective Manager' and I was appointed as academic advisor and invited to write the text of much of the course. The Open University is based on home study so I saw this as a wonderful opportunity to tie the classroom teaching to the day to day work experiences of the students who were all working in some form of organisation – earning while learning, I was pleased to note. It was also valuable learning for me. I was a member of a course team, the only academic member in fact. The others included the editors of the published texts that we were creating, the writers and producers of the accompanying television broadcasts, the organisers of the summer school that would come at the end of the course, the financial controllers, the marketing and sales people as well as sundry others from time to time who all had a stake in the process and the outcome.

No one ever disputed my versions of the relevant theories but they had a constant refrain when they read the material I submitted: 'Why would they want to turn the page?' they asked, pointing out that the students would be studying at home after a long day's work. The material had to grab their interest. It had to be relevant, interesting, even exciting if they were to absorb it. I was being hoist with my own petard, forced to hold true to my own beliefs that the concepts must connect with experience. Moreover I was being judged by a very tough bunch of colleagues whose work depended on my contributions. It was the hardest thing I had ever done but it forced me to examine everything I wrote to see whether it was, in fact, relevant and useful. The course we constructed together was a success. It became the cornerstone of the Open Business School, which now has more students in its programmes than any other business school in Europe. The combination theory works.

A few years later, in 1987, I built on this experience when chairing the report 'The Making of Managers', which compared and contrasted the very different ways in which Britain, America, France, Germany and Japan educated their managers. It was clear that each country followed their own educational traditions. America did it in classrooms, Germany in prolonged university study, Japan inside the mega corporations and France in their *grandes écoles*. Why, I questioned, did Britain alone disregard their own tradition and follow the Americans? I advocated a two-part MBA degree. The first part, to be taken before or immediately after joining an organisation, would cover what I called the Language of Business, to be studied in the classroom. This would be equivalent to the first part of a doctor's degree in medicine or the part one of an architectural qualification. The second part of the MBA would come later and would be related to current experience, would be part time and would involve mentors from the participants' organisations.

This was too radical a proposal for the time but in a rather muddled way it has happened. The proliferation of undergraduate courses in Business Studies are the equivalent of my Part One, while the growth of part-time programmes for working executives has opened the way for more use of some combination of practice and theory. The British have slowly felt their way back to their early traditions.

These reflections came later, however – too late for the London version of the Sloan programme that I had returned from America to create and direct. Nonetheless I was determined that it would have to be as good as the MIT programme but with some added benefits. I hoped to find a way to include some parts of that Oxford introduction to philosophical thinking that I was finding increasingly valuable as my life went on. Oxford plus MIT, I felt, could be a powerful combination.

Chapter Seven
The Antigone Challenge

In September 1968 the executive students on the Sloan programme at the London Business School were excited, curious and just a touch apprehensive. It was the first day of what was then a new approach to management education and they were the guinea pigs. They entered the classroom to find two books in front of each of their seats. One was called The Meaning of Company Accounts – the sort of thing they had come for – but the other raised their eyebrows a little. It was the tragedy Antigone, written by Sophocles in the fifth century BC (in translation, I hasten to add). The book was a symbol of my wish, as programme director, to broaden the scope of executive education to embrace values as well as techniques. More than that, it was an expression of my unease with the culture of business, an unease that has only increased over the years.

The programme was a big risk for the new school. As I went around the lunch tables of the corporations looking for recruits I was uncomfortably aware that, until then, the longest formal management programme on offer in Britain was just one day long. Yet I was asking these firms to send me one of their best and brightest for nine months, to pay us a fee but also to keep their nominee on full salary plus expenses. They would have to take a lot on trust. The school, after all, was only two years old and had not yet graduated any students, and I would be younger than most of them. On reflection I was fortunate to find eighteen out of my target of twenty.

That first morning was, therefore, something of an experiment for all of us. When I was designing the programme I was conscious that, back then, even successful young executives were often financially illiterate. They could not easily decipher a corporate balance sheet, and probably had not as yet had need to do so, buried as they had been in the depths of some corporate function where their task had been to carry out their assigned role without bothering themselves about the financial details of the business as a whole. Now that they were, supposedly, on their way to senior management roles, our first duty was to remedy this serious gap. Hence that first book on their tables, *The Meaning of Company Accounts*.

But I also wanted them to be thinking businessmen (as at MIT, they were all males in that first year). I wanted to encourage them to question the world they found themselves in, to work out their own priorities in life and work, to be their own people, not the slaves of their employers. These students would be philosopher-managers if I had anything to do with it. That Oxford experience of mine had sunk deep. Hence *Antigone*, which was the first of what would be a weekly piece of literature to be discussed as a group. This part of the programme was, I suppose, a sort of 'Great Books' experience or, as I saw it, an introduction to Socratic thinking. The sessions were led by a fascinating character, one Bill Letwin, an American economist working at the LSE whom I had encountered at MIT. Bill had developed his own way of drawing out philosophical and ethical issues from books that ranged from Plato's *Republic* and Sophocles' tragedies to more modern classics such as *Billy Budd* and *Heart of Darkness*. We even took our students to the theatre to see *King Lear* and *Othello*, to be discussed the next day in the classroom.

Antigone seemed a good piece to start with. In Sophocles' tragedy, Antigone is forced to choose between the orders of her uncle, the ruler of Thebes, and her conscience, her duty to her gods. Kreon, the uncle, had just killed her brother in a battle for control of the city and had issued an edict that his nephew's body was to lie unburied outside the walls for the crows and the vultures to pick at. To Antigone this was to condemn her brother to perpetual hell; according to her religion, souls that were not put to rest would be chased forever by the Furies. It was Antigone's duty to her brother to bury him. But Kreon had decreed that anyone disobeying his order would be executed and her duty as a citizen was to obey her uncle's order. To Antigone the choice was no choice. She had to do what was right by her religion and her brother. So she did and so she died.

Would our executives have done the same in her place? That was the question we put to them. Did they hold any beliefs so dear that they would disobey orders, no matter what the consequences? What, a visiting bishop once asked them, was their sticking point? Should private morality ever prevail against legitimate authority? Should a good person obey a bad law, or a bad order? Old philosophical questions, maybe, but new to most of them. They were questions, I felt, that were often ignored by businesses that believed that their ends justified all means, provided they were technically legal – or undetectable. This was before the days of concepts such as corporate social responsibility and of the scandals of Enron and World Com and the like, scandals that were, with hindsight, quite predictable given the prevailing culture of business where the ends justified most means.

Few of us are ever faced with such a cruel dilemma as Antigone. Equivalent dilemmas do, however, kick in at lower levels. Most of us grow up being assured that our elders know best, that those in authority have the right to expect us to do what they say, that professionals of all sorts know what they are doing and can be trusted to tell us what to do, what can be done and what can't. Doctors, architects, lawyers and financial advisors – I am predisposed to accept what they say even though I know that they are only human, can't be always right, and that some seem downright stupid when they are outside their area of expertise. I used to think that government ministers were likely to get things right, what with all their advisors, until some of my students ended up in those jobs, and I knew they weren't always that clever or that wise. I once almost believed our plumber when he told me that to put our garden tap over a drain was against building regulations, until common sense took over and I realised that he was just too lazy to move it. I have learnt from painful experience that although professionals may know more of the answers than I do, it is important that I know what questions to ask them. It was one of the lessons I hoped my students would learn from our course.

If we take our faith in the expertise of others too far we can end up handing over control of our lives to people we do not know. We once employed a woman to clean our house. She was the wife of a soldier and lived in army quarters. Sadly, she told us one day that she and her husband were going to get divorced. She would have to leave their army house. Where would she live? I asked. 'They haven't told me yet,' she replied.

Wondering who would take responsibility for housing the ex-wives of soldiers, I asked her, 'Who are "they"?'

She looked at me as if I was amazingly stupid, 'They haven't told me yet who they are, have they?' The possibility that there was no longer any 'they' looking after her had not occurred to her. Nor did she believe me when I suggested that it might be so.

'They' might be the government or the management team or authority in general. Some are willing to give them almost total responsibility for our moral behaviour. As one person put it to me, 'If it was wrong they would have made it illegal, wouldn't they? As far as I'm concerned, anything legal must be OK.' But, with some exceptions at the extreme, it is not illegal to be personally cruel, to commit adultery, to lie, to overcharge for a product or service, to reveal a confidence or to connive in someone's deceit. We should not want to delegate all moral decisions to government. That is to give them a responsibility they neither want nor deserve. It is inconceivable that Antigone would have allowed Kreon to take the moral decision on her behalf.

Yet, much of the time, most of us are ethically lazy. It is easier to do what we are asked without questioning it too much if someone in a white coat or a serious-looking badge is doing the asking. To accompany *Antigone* I also showed my students a film of Stanley Milgram's experiment. Milgram, an American social scientist, set out to explore how far we would go in accepting authority. He asked a number of volunteer subjects to act as teachers of people trying to learn a series of simple word pairs. The anonymous, and studiously neutral, white-coated administrator told them that they were to punish the students when they got it wrong by administering an electric shock. At first the shocks were minor, but at each mistake the power of the shock was increased. The 'teacher' was separated from the 'learner' by a partition but could see the level of the shock he was administering on a dial. He could also hear, though not see, the learner. Even when the learner screamed in agony, the teacher would continue to administer a shock at the bidding of the administrator, right up to where the dial clearly read 'Fatal'. At this level two out of three teachers were still applying the shocks.

In actual fact there were no shocks administered and the screams were false, but it was clear from the film that the experimental subjects did not suspect this. They went about their assigned task with the utmost seriousness, determined to do their best to satisfy the white-coated authority. What was horrific, however, on the film, was to observe the methodical way the teachers pressed the lever despite the agonised screams that could clearly be heard. Only when Milgram put another lot of subjects in a group and employed two accomplices who set an example by refusing to obey their instructions did the level of disobedience rise. Even then, however, one third of the subjects still obeyed.

Milgram's experiment seemed to explain how and why the guards at the Nazi concentration camps obeyed their obscene orders. It may explain why the soldiers accused of abusing prisoners in Iraq felt that to say they were only obeying orders was a sufficient explanation for their behaviour. It may even explain why, when I started work in Malaysia, where I worked for one of only two oil companies, I so readily and complacently accepted the argument that to fix the prices of government tenders between us was good for everyone.

It was an argument that I also went along with some years later in the interlude between leaving Shell and going to America in 1965. I was acting as secretary to three very large men, from America, South Africa and Belgium, when they met in Paris to fix the producer copper price for that year. At the time, I was working for one of the three biggest copper producers in the world, of which those large men were the sales managers. They met at regular intervals, rather like OPEC in later years, except that these were independent businesses not countries, to agree on a figure at which each of their firms would sell their copper. The intention was to stabilise the price across the industry, at a level, naturally, that also guaranteed them a satisfactory profit. I felt that they were acting possibly illegally and certainly against the spirit of free trade, but I kept my head down, said nothing and enjoyed helping them later decide which three-star restaurant we would dine at that evening.

We may think that we, too, would be like Henry Fonda in another film we showed on that course, *Twelve Angry Men*, in which Fonda stood out against the other eleven members of a jury and ultimately converted them to his view, but in practice, few of us care enough and, anyway, Fonda's job was not at stake – only his integrity. How much do we each value that integrity, I wonder, when the pressure builds? We have to admire all those who stick to their beliefs under torture when they have nothing to gain and everything to lose. It is people such as these we call martyrs, and it is hardly surprising that there are so few of them. Of course, we first have to be sure that we know what our beliefs are – but that is an issue for another chapter.

Torture does not have to be physical, as anyone can testify who has ever raised a hand to point out an abuse. You have to be resilient and courageous to be a whistle-blower, even privately within the organisation, or to stick up for your beliefs in the community. No one will thank you. You will almost certainly lose your job, or at the very least be ostracised by your fellows or fail to be promoted. 'We don't tolerate whistle-blowers here,' one chief executive said to me. At least he was honest, although you had to wonder what he was afraid of. The world may admire the truth-tellers, but few will want to employ them.

I wonder now why I didn't protest at what my employers were doing in their collaboration with their competitors. It was because, perhaps, I didn't see it as a moral issue, or, more likely, because I didn't want to offend my bosses. Others are not so cowardly. In 2005 Dr David Graham was an employee of the Food and Drug Administration in the USA. He felt it his moral duty to go to the media and publicly criticise his organisation's failure to act decisively on evidence that Vioxx, an arthritis drug taken by twenty million Americans, had caused heart attacks or death in up to 140,000 patients in five years. His Catholic faith had driven him to reveal what he knew. He is still employed by the FDA, but, 'I am not considered part of the family any more,' he said. 'This whole thing has been quite an experience.' A quiet understatement I suspect, but, to be fair to the FDA, he was not dismissed.

One of the worst crimes at my school was to be a sneak – to tell on your mates. Almost as unpopular was to defy the group norms, to be different. In retrospect I could have given my students William Golding's *Lord of the Flies* to read, that tale of a group of boys, marooned on an island, who hype themselves up and become a single organism, one in which the individual loses his own identity and with it any sense of individual responsibility. It is behaviour that, these days, can be seen in Britain's city centres at weekends when half-drunken youths, of both sexes, pour out of the pubs, hyped up, with their own identity subsumed in that of the group, no longer seemingly responsible for their own behaviour.

In business the same phenomenon can be seen, only a little more positively, in start-up situations or in some aggressive merger and acquisition campaigns. In the excitement of the chase a group ethos develops, one in which the ethical niceties can sometimes be over-whelmed by the desire to win or succeed. Corners are cut, distinctions blurred, right and wrong redefined as what will work and what won't. Tom Wolfe, in *The Bonfire of the Vanities*, describes how it was in the go-go eighties in New York, when the standards were set by the swash-buckling kings of Wall Street, the self-styled Masters of the Universe, to whom money was god and greed was good. Many must have squirmed inwardly as they did what was expected of them at this time, sacrificing any qualms they might feel. But they still did it. Michael Lewis describes the scene well in his book *Liar's Poker*:

> As a Salomon Brothers' trainee, of course, you didn't worry too much about ethics. You were just trying to stay alive. You felt flat-tered to be on the same team with the people who kicked everyone's ass all the time. Like a kid mysteriously befriended by the playground bully you tended to overlook the flaws of bond people in return for their protection.

Another kind of ethical blurring can happen in great corporations, or at the top of governments. Archbishop Tutu once said regretfully that President Mbeki of South Africa had been surrounded by a 'sycophantic, hubristic' cabal of henchmen who were separating him from his people and, he hinted, from his previous values and aims. President Mbeki is not the only head of state to risk losing touch with his earlier beliefs as they get immersed in events and surrounded by overeager allies. His neighbour in Zimbabwe is a more conspicuous example. It is the seductive corruption of power.

'The same,' says author Edward Luttwak, 'is true of corporate chief-tains, surrounded by deferential staff, grandly transported in personal jets, courted by politicians in need of campaign contributions, by heads of universities proffering honorary degrees, even by foreign ministers and presidents eager to attract investments, the chiefs of the biggest US corporations could easily acquire Napoleonic pretensions.' That they don't, he suggests, is largely due to the threat of legal actions by the voracious tigers of the American legal system. The law is once again acting as the substitute for personal morality.

My own attempt to introduce some ideas of ethical philosophy into management education did not last long. The students and their companies wanted something with a more immediate payback. The utilitarian prevailed over the philosophical, as it often does. Later in my time at the business school I offered an optional class in Ethics to the MBA students. Few signed up. As one of them explained, 'I would love to do your course, Professor, but later, after I have got a job. Right now International Finance is a more important subject, I'm afraid.'

I couldn't blame him. I knew myself how necessity narrows our horizons. The need to secure the next step stops us looking to see where the path is leading or what we are missing by not looking around us as we travel. In the end, in my own need to fill the places on the programme, I succumbed to the pressures of the market, as expressed in the wishes of the students, and curtailed Bill Letwin's group discussions. Later, looking back, I wondered whether that very market was not itself one of the pressures for conformity.

Should one follow the market or try to lead it? Is the customer always right, or are others better placed to know what is likely to be best for them? Should one follow the consensus or have the confidence to do what you believe to be better? It isn't always an easy decision. In business, I knew, successful entrepreneurs and innovative organisations are those who back their own ideas against the going fashion, but they are only risking their own money. If one does the same in education the risk falls on the students. If I had ignored the priorities of my students I would have been accused of arrogance and might not have filled subsequent programmes. But was I being a coward and a traitor to myself when I discarded something I believed to be in their best interests? I am still not sure. Sometimes it is indeed arrogance to trust your views more than those of others. Great leaders seem to live with a mix of humility and confidence, which includes the ability to admit on occasion that they are wrong.

These decisions are easier, paradoxically, when the issues are moral ones, as in Antigone's case, even if the consequences are tougher. No one has the right to challenge your deepest beliefs and convictions. The decisions are yours alone. Only you can weigh up the private costs of denying yourself against the very obvious pains of sticking to your truth. The decisions are trickier when it is more a practical matter of what will work best. How far should you push something when the stakes are small? Standing up for your ideas, acting in accordance with your own values and convictions may not always seem to be worth the cost, particularly when you are trying to win friends and influence others in your environment. It is so much easier to go with the flow, except that the stream may eventually, and almost imperceptibly, carry you to a place where you never meant to be.

When I chose *Antigone* to open that first executive programme I had not expected it to infiltrate my own life and thinking in the way that it subsequently did. But that, no doubt, is the reason why Sophocles' short play is still read and performed two-and-a-half thousand years after it was written. Great art worms its way into the soul, in a way that company accounts never can. Had it all been a waste of time, I asked myself at the end of it? No, not really. It had been a pleasure and a privilege to try to assist the growth and education of some highly competent people who were eager to learn, and very demanding. I once arrived ten minutes late for a session to find the class calculating the refund due to them on their fees. I had also confirmed my belief that the surest way to learn something is to try teaching it. I am sure, therefore, that I learnt more than my students. And a lot of it had been fun, as it nearly always is when you are working with intelligent people on problems of mutual interest.

At the end of it I was more than ever convinced that while the skills of business analysis can be taught in class or learnt from books, the art and practice of management cannot. Management will always be largely a matter of acquired common sense and each individual will have to discover what approach will work best for them. The personal skills that are needed can best be developed by careful mentoring, and, more usually, by trial and error. It will always be useful to reflect upon those trials, and particularly those errors. That is, ultimately, how we all learn, from childhood onwards. Sometimes that reflection can best be done in the company of strangers in secluded surroundings with the assistance of trained interpreters. Executive programmes, at their best, offer that opportunity, but to suggest that passing their examinations in some way qualifies anyone as a manager is to exaggerate dangerously.

Chapter Eight
My Father's Death

When I was forty-nine years old I received a letter from the BBC. They wanted me to take part in a series of programmes on BBC Television called 'The Light of Experience'. It was, for them, television on the cheap. They invited individuals who had gone through a life-changing experience to talk about it straight to camera, without an interviewer, and to illustrate their story with their own photographs. There was, I remember, a barrister who had married her convicted murderer client in his cell and a woman who had been in a Thai prison for years having been caught drug smuggling. My life, I told the BBC, had been a dull monochrome affair compared with these colourful, even exotic, examples. My life-changing experience had been something so ordinary that everyone had experienced it. It was the death of my father. 'That's why we want you,' they said, 'because it is something that everyone can relate to.'

Foolishly, I agreed, because it was, as I soon discovered, fiendishly difficult to speak directly to camera, reading from an autocue, and still look human. Newsreaders clearly have the art that conceals art because they make it seem so effortless and natural. When I watched the eventual programme I thought I looked like a stuffed penguin, sitting in a chair glaring ahead. This, however, was the story I told. I have set it down before, but because it was the major turning point or hinge in my life, I need to recall it here.

I was on my way back from an international conference in Paris when I got a message to say that my father had suffered a crippling stroke and was dying in a Dublin hospital. It was a shock. We tend to assume that parents will go on forever and he had only retired from his work as a Church of Ireland minister two years before. Meantime I had been living the vaguely glamorous life of a business academic, jetting hither and yon, books published, busy, busy, climbing my career ladder as fast as I could. But he was seventy-four and I knew that he had experienced some small heart problems in recent years. I rushed back to Ireland to be with my mother and sisters at his bedside. He died the day after I got there having never regained consciousness.

It was sad. I had been fond of my father. He was a quiet, gentle and kindly man. I loved the way he took the services in church but, at home, I never really knew his inmost thoughts. He was private in many ways; to tell the truth I was a little disappointed in him. He should not, I felt, have been content to stay in the same small country parish for most of his working life, turning down opportunities for promotion or even the invitations to move to a larger city parish where, selfishly, I could have had more fun. He seemed a man without ambition.

In Ireland it is customary to have a funeral no more than two days after the death, so we hurriedly arranged to take him back to the parish church some twenty miles outside Dublin where he had ministered to his small group of Protestant parishioners for forty years. It would be a simple family affair, a quiet ending for a quiet man, although we did put a notice in the papers for the next day.

We, the family, followed the hearse down the main road from Dublin. I don't think any of us said much. It was a sad journey down a well-remembered road. Then something odd happened: as we approached the turn-off to our village, a police car came out from the side of the road, halted the oncoming traffic and started to escort the hearse along the side road. What was happening? We hadn't asked for this. Then as we approached our old church, set deep in the countryside, we found the road lined with cars for hundreds of yards. Luckily, someone had kept places for us. And the church itself was full, overflowing in fact. People were standing outside, lining the path. We went inside, wondering. The choir came in, dressed as always in black cassocks and white surplices, but the robes were very obviously far too small. These weren't the usual choirboys; they were, we began to realise, the old choirboys who had spontaneously decided to come back from all over Ireland to sit in the choir once more – for my father.

And the archbishop, my father's old boss, was there, too, walking behind them in full Episcopal regalia. Strange – we had believed him to be in hospital. But he had discharged himself and travelled down especially to be there. My father, he told the congregation, had been a special man who had helped very many and had earned the admiration of even more. His life and ministry were an example to all.

Outside, as we stood beside the open grave after they had lowered his coffin, people, so many people, came up to us. 'Your father baptised me,' one said, 'he celebrated our marriage in this church and a few years ago he baptised my daughter. He was a big part of our family.' 'He gave me such wise advice at a critical time in my life,' another said, 'he seemed so in touch with the world.' Others just said, 'We will miss him. There aren't many like him.'

I stood there pondering this man whom I suddenly realised I had never understood. How many people would come to my funeral, I asked myself? The grapevine must have been very active for so many to drop everything at one day's notice and get here from all over. To whom did my life and work matter that much? What price my busy life and so-called achievements in comparison with all these lives that he had so obviously affected? This was no ordinary man. It was my problem, not his. I had been judging him in the wrong way.

I went away both sorrowful and thoughtful. I had been losing myself in all my busyness. If I was going to matter to anyone else I must rediscover my true self. It was, I began to see, tempting but misguided to accept the values and aspirations of others instead of working them out for yourself.

I was later to discover that most of us need pain and trauma, or rejection and disappointment, to trigger a change of life. 'We don't have careers any more,' a young Irishman said to me not so long ago, 'we have lives, several of them in our lifespan.' Indeed, but to switch lives takes courage. It is much easier to stay with the one you know even if it does not seem to be going anywhere. Changing lives can often involve starting at the bottom of another ladder, but if you have just discovered that the ladder that you were climbing is leaning up against the wrong wall then the decision is really made for you. You badly need to find another ladder, soon. It is, however, one thing mentally to take the decision, quite another to make it operational.

In the years that followed my father's death I have talked with a wide range of people who have done quite well in life. Many of them have a similar tale of pain or shock to recount, something that jolted them onto another path. It might be a rejection, a failure to get a particular job or promotion. For some it was redundancy, a shock at the time, and one that is always taken personally even if it was not intended as such. Looking back, later, the imposed departure was often seen as a welcome release from a dead end. A close encounter with death, one's own, or, as in my case, someone close to you, was a frequent story.

Marriage breakdown was another, a death of a sort. One successful banker had ticked all the boxes by his early thirties: 'I had it all – the house in the country with tennis courts, pool and lake, four children and a gorgeous wife with her own Porsche, then I came home one weekend to find her having an affair with another man. On reflection, I had been away so much and when I was at home I probably took her too much for granted and focused what time I had on the children. I was a good father but a poor husband.' They divorced and a year later he left his job to go into full-time charity work. 'The end of my marriage,' he said, 'made me look afresh at where my life was heading and I didn't like it much.'

It often does require such a trigger to start the second curve of life. I developed the theory of the sigmoid (or S-shaped) curves to explain how a business grows, yet can ultimately fail, but the curves apply equally well to our own lives. The first sigmoid curve demonstrates how almost everything, from empires to organisations to products, starts by taking in more than it gives out. In business this is the investment that every new venture needs. As individuals we call this our education. Then, all being well, the output builds up, the firm grows, success beckons. Inevitably, however, what worked so well at first sometime later falters as better or cheaper rivals catch up. The curve turns down until failure looms. It is only then that most businesses begin desperately to think about alternatives. Too often it is too late. This is the first sigmoid curve:

It would be better by far, obviously, to do that thinking before the turn down began, to start a second curve before the first one peaked, at point A, like this:

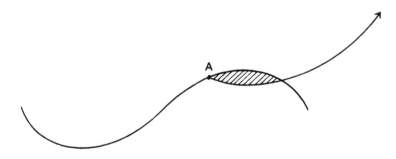

This is obvious in retrospect, but it is far from clear at the time. At that point in the first curve everything looks set fair. Things are going well. If something isn't broken we don't fix it. By the time people realise that things are no longer going so well they have spent the reserves they had, are frightened, stressed and depressed. Only a major restructuring can save them, a restructuring that turns out to be a comfortable euphemism for halving the staff or selling the business to a competitor.

It is no easier for individuals. The right time to think about developing a new life, to start a new job or a new interest, is when things are still going well. That is as hard for an individual as it is for an organisation, or a political party come to that. Only a shock of the sort I have been talking about can jerk one out of complacency. The question I am always asked when describing these curves is, 'How does one know when one is at point A?' One never does, except in retrospect, which doesn't help. But there are some clues. Comfort is one. If you feel totally comfortable and in command of your life or work, you may be mistaking the illusion of security for complacency. It is always dangerous to rest on one's laurels, in private life as in business.

It is because it is so hard to leave while the party is still going strong that we need that trigger, that shock, however painful it may be. At that point it is hard to believe that there will ever be another curve as good as the one you are on. But as one door closes another opens, often a door we had not noticed before, or had ignored because we were so busy with that first curve. Chris Patten, the British politician, lost his parliamentary seat in the 1992 general election. At the time he was chairman of the Conservative Party and likely to be chancellor of the exchequer if the Conservatives won, which they did. It must have been one of the blackest days of his life. His whole life had been in politics and now, on the threshold of high office, it had ended, at least for a while. Yet, a year later, he was governor of Hong Kong with the task of handing it over to the Chinese as the lease of that territory came to an end. It was, he later said, the best job he ever had or could have had. A second curve had been granted to him, unsought, a curve that he would have let pass by unnoticed had he not just been cast into the political wilderness.

We can't all be so lucky with our next life, but less exotically, those who suffer from redundancy but then go on to other things often say that they wish they had done it years earlier. Some do. It was recently revealed that one third of Britain's new teachers came from successful careers in other spheres, mostly business. They had left, they said, because they wanted a more intellectual and socially useful challenge. As the old idea of a long seamless career in one occupation is seen as the myth that it now is, it will become more common for people to think of having two or three very different lives, often needing very different skills and with different forms of reward. You could see it as giving us all the chance of reincarnation without the need for a physical death.

As for me, I went away from my father's funeral determined to change my life. That day had been the trigger, even though it took a whole year to make it happen. My first thought was to follow my father into the ordained ministry, to become the kind of priest that he had been, the strong caring pillar of a community. I invited two bishops that I knew to supper. Would they, I asked, be willing to support my application to enter a theological college, the first step on the journey to ordination?

Somewhat to my surprise, they refused. I might, they suggested, be quite a good bishop but I would never get that far. I would be hopeless, they said, as an inner-city curate, the first level of the priesthood and one that I would be unlikely to survive. I recognised, reluctantly, that they were right. I did not have the skills or the temperament to deal with the traumas and difficulties of those at the bottom of society's pyramid. But, they said, there is a job that you could do and which might satisfy your wish to work within the church. The job of warden of St George's House in Windsor Castle was, they said, currently vacant, although applications were closing in a week's time.

I knew the job they were referring to. St George's House was a small conference and study centre set inside Windsor Castle in some of the old residences of the canons of St George's Chapel. It had a twofold mission: to prepare the clergy for senior roles in the Church, and to run consultations on some of the ethical and moral issues in society. I had myself taken part in one or two of these meetings and knew what was involved. The warden was the quaint name for the head of this mini institution. The first two wardens had been admirals. There was a feeling, my two bishops said, that someone from a more academic background would bring a fresh approach to what was, in effect, a place that was concerned to connect Christian teaching with the realities of society. They encouraged me to apply. I did and, to my rather embarrassed surprise, was offered the job. When you test the waters you don't necessarily mean to swim.

So now came the crunch. This was for real, no longer just a theoretical possibility. Did I really want to leave my comfortable tenured professorship for a five-year appointment with no obvious place to go to afterwards? Besides, there was the money. At first I thought that they were offering me the equivalent of my professor's salary, then in the order of £3,500 per month. Later, looking more closely at the badly typed small print in the contract document, I saw that the figure they had quoted was p.a. not p.m.! Yes, there would be a rather grand free house provided, and free heating and electricity, but I had two young children to feed and educate as well as my wife and myself on a salary that would be less than ten per cent of the not particularly generous pay of an academic.

This was starting at the bottom again all right. My wife, however, was determined that it was the right thing to do. I remembered, then, how a couple of years before she had wondered why I gave so much of my time and energy to my business school students instead of to her and our children. 'You are only helping to make spoilt rich kids richer,' she said, 'you could be doing something more worthwhile.' I protested that I was educating the future leaders of the country, but I suspected that she was right. A change, any change, she felt, would be an escape from what had become a trap. Twenty years earlier, leaving my home in an Irish vicarage, I had promised myself two things: I would never go to church again, and I would never be poor again. Yet here I was, about to sign up for a way of life in which I knew that I would be expected to go to St George's Chapel every day and would be living on the equivalent of my father's salary. The past has an uncomfortable way of catching up on you.

It turned out to be the best decision I could have made. It launched me into another, wider, world. We survived financially, too. My wife let out our London apartment and the income helped to pay for the groceries. It was enough. I left four years later – to step into an empty void and to start what was, in effect, my fourth life. But that is another story.

Chapter Nine
Home Is a Castle

I arrived at Windsor Castle with my family in September 1977 to take up my appointment as warden of St George's House. I didn't like the title. It sounded as if I was looking after an old folks' home, but I had liked the sound of the job, running what I saw as a think tank on social and ethical issues. I was also, I confess, intrigued by the thought of living inside Windsor Castle, having explored the house that went with the job.

Windsor Castle was perhaps England's strangest village. Seventy families lived there, one of them the Queen's. Our new neighbours included her private secretary and her librarian, as well as the Dean of St George's Chapel, the adult choristers and, importantly, the castle plumber. An intriguing and even exotic mix, all nicely arranged in order on the hill inside the walls, the noblest 'up top' as everyone called it, the singers and craftsmen at the bottom, only just below me. Come Christmastime we would go carol singing round the castle homes, led by the chapel choir, and would end up singing to the Queen, surrounded by her corgis, with very welcome trays of mulled wine to refresh us. I was an oddity there, too young to have the kinds of campaign medals that everyone else sported on ritual occasions and too academic for some tastes – when I used the word 'economics' in one of my early papers I was told not to use jargon that no one could understand. Challenged to say what the word meant, I found it hard to do at all crisply. Point taken.

Our new home, 25 The Cloisters, was a sprawling residence in the old wall of the castle, built around the remains of Henry III's palace of the thirteenth century. King John, I used to speculate, probably mounted his horse in our courtyard as he left for Runnymede to sign Magna Carta. Our bedroom was open to the public, by appointment, because it had once been used as the practice room for the choir of the chapel in the sixteenth century and the music was still painted on the walls. It was undoubtedly the most unusual and grand house that we have ever lived in. The only problem was that it was large and came unfurnished. When I received the estimate for the carpets and curtains it came to more than my annual salary.

However, that was the least of my problems. I had failed to do my due diligence before accepting the post and had only a vague idea of what the situation was or what my job really entailed. St George's House was an integral part of the centuries-old College of St George, built around St George's Chapel. It had been founded ten years earlier by Prince Philip and the then Dean of Windsor, Robin Woods, in order to make good use of the two vacant canons' houses in the courtyard behind the chapel. Their idea was that the house should be a meeting place for people of influence in society, including particularly ministers of religion, to discuss the important ethical and social issues of the day. They had raised the money from business for the necessary restorations. The Dean and canons of the chapel would act as an associate faculty but the day-to-day running of the house would be in the hands of a warden and a director of studies, both laypeople.

My idea that, as warden, I was going to be the boss turned out to be an illusion, as it often does in organisations. There is always someone or some group above you. In my case it was, firstly, the Dean who was in charge of all that happened in the chapel bit of the castle, except that he was not all-powerful either. He was only the chairman of the Chapter, a body comprised of the canons who together with him bore the ultimate responsibility under the Charter of Edward IV. I had not realised that I was going to be part of such a medieval tangle. Then there was the Council of the House on which sat Prince Philip, three knights of the garter, including at least one ex-prime minister, and others of the great and the good. I was in a real life chess game, I sometimes felt, surrounded by a queen and her castle with bishops and knights, and myself as one of the pawns. It was all a rather top-heavy structure for such a tiny operation employing some dozen persons in all. That is often the way with organisations – lots of chiefs, too few Indians.

Those on top might have all the say, but it was still I and my colleagues who had to deliver. In my first week I received two shocks. On the first day the bursar, who looked after the food and lodgings, told me that there was not enough money in the bank to pay that week's wages for the domestic staff. I had been assured by one of the canons that the place was adequately funded so this was an unexpected problem. I went down to the bank, just outside the castle, to introduce myself and ask for an overdraft to see us through the immediate predicament. 'I'm sure that will not be a problem,' the manager said, 'what security would you like to provide?'

I pointed out of the window to the big bulk of the castle. 'Won't that be enough?' I said, a little smugly.

He smiled. 'Not valid, I'm afraid, unless you hold the deeds.' He did provide me with some temporary help but I walked slowly back pondering the fact that I had inherited a bankrupt organisation.

The following day my secretary placed a large calendar for the next year in front of me. 'You need to plan the year,' she said.

'But there's nothing here except dates,' I said, 'isn't there anything already planned?'

'Not yet,' she smiled (why did everybody in Windsor smile when they gave me bad news?). 'We were waiting for you.' It was my job to fill in the proposed discussions and events for the year. There were some regular events that could, no doubt, be repeated, but much of the space on that calendar was up for grabs. It was a stark reminder that we needed urgently to work out what the strategy of the organisation was, or, in simpler English, what we were there for.

But first we had to take care of our finances or we wouldn't survive. The place was shabby, the income inadequate, because it all came from the tiny fees we charged those attending our discussions. We did, however, have a unique asset, a small conference facility inside Windsor Castle, including a meeting room in which, it was said, Shakespeare had once directed *The Merry Wives of Windsor* in front of Elizabeth I. My new colleague, John Long, Director of Studies, and myself had many connections with business. We believed that businesses would be eager to hire the place for small away-days or corporate retreats and would pay serious money. So indeed it proved. By the end of the first year it was clear that we could run a very profitable enterprise by renting it out to corporations.

But was this what we were there for? Obviously not, but it was tempting, looking at that bottom line. Who says that charitable organisations don't need profits? It's just that they call them 'operating surpluses' and put them in reserves. We knew, however, that maximising those surpluses was definitely not what we were there for. We had to be careful to restrict our more commercial activities to cover only what was needed to keep us going. We had to make sure that we had enough but not more than enough to do our real job.

But what was enough? That old Aristotle question once again. We paid ourselves minimal salaries, in line with our clerical colleagues, although it was barely enough to live on. The same went for the secretaries and the domestic staff who were paid only the minimum that the law allowed. If we increased our commercial lettings we could pay ourselves and our staff decent wages, as well as making the whole place more luxurious, but then we would be rightly accused of running the place for our own benefit, not for that of our clientele. How much simpler it would be, I felt, if we were an ordinary business. Making money is not that difficult if you don't care how you make it or what you do with it. I began slowly to realise that I was living the capitalist dilemma. Money, and profit, is essential to the survival and growth of any enterprise, but if it is the only or even the main purpose, it will be seen as selfish and may lead to a neglect of the wider responsibilities that business owes to society. What those wider business responsibilities might be would be the subject of some of our subsequent discussions with our invited participants.

I don't like or approve of begging. I believe that, wherever possible, charities should earn their own income because only in that way can they be self-sustaining and have control over their future. Yes, they will need support from time to time, especially in the early days. They should also be able to borrow money or to solicit investment like any business, even if the investment provides psychological rather than financial returns for the investors. In many situations their income, or part of it, will come from government in return for doing some socially useful work for them, but in other cases they will need to develop a business arm to their charity work, as we were forced to do at Windsor. Apart from the useful income, the need to be fully commercial in some parts of the operation does instill a degree of managerial discipline.

The dilemma I encountered at St George's House stood me in good stead ten years later when I ran into a similar problem as chairman of the Royal Society of Arts, or more properly the Royal Society for the Encouragement of Arts and Manufactures. This was and is a venerable eighteenth-century charity housed in a splendid set of Adam buildings off the Strand in London. Its purpose is to stimulate progress in society through the discussion and promulgation of new ideas, to launch pilot projects and to celebrate the pioneers. It all costs money. There are twenty-two thousand Fellows whose subscriptions help but are not enough on their own. The balance was provided in the past by income from one of the early projects of the society, the RSA Examinations, which were taken by vocational students around the world. This income allowed the society to be comfortably self-supporting.

Too comfortable to last. The year before I took over we were obliged to hive off RSA Examinations in order to allow it to be an independent examinations authority in line with the government's reforms to the system. I inherited a society facing a deficit on its operations for the first time in recent history. Was this the Windsor experience again, I wondered? There were, however, some splendid vaults below the society's house, rented out to a wine merchant for an unduly modest rent. The council of the society discussed the possibility of turning the vaults into a set of dining and meeting rooms that would then make it feasible to rent out the facilities of the whole house as a conference location.

It would cost five million pounds, money we did not have. We would have to beg or borrow it. I argued that to beg for an investment that would allow us to make money, and thus make the society self-sustaining, was more acceptable to givers than begging for running costs and that we could borrow any shortfall by mortgaging our buildings. Sitting at the head of the council table, I was intrigued by the range of attitudes around the room. There were some who thought it beneath the dignity of the society to hire itself out. They disliked the thought of indiscriminate strangers using our facilities. Others felt that renting out our facilities was a distortion of our objectives and a distraction from our charitable purpose. I could sympathise with both views, but needs must when the red ink shows. More surprising were the attitudes of the business people at the table. They felt that we should not do it unless and until we could finance it out of income, that it would be hard to raise the money and foolhardy to mortgage our buildings. How, I wondered, did they run their own businesses without investment or borrowings?

At this point I engaged in a little furtive manipulation. In the crucial council debate, after all the arguments pro and con had been discussed,

I went round the table asking each member in turn to signal their approval or disapproval of the proposal, but I had so arranged the seating that those whom I knew would be in favour voted first. When it came to the diehard opposers it was clear to each of them that they would be outvoted, so, to preserve harmony, they abstained. I was able to declare that the motion had been carried *nem. con.* Is it a legitimate form of leadership to stage-manage things in such a way in order to achieve what you sincerely believe to be right? I am still not sure.

So, with a few misgivings, the council had agreed. The resulting transformation of the vaults has been the financial underpinning of the society, as well as providing a stylish addition to its facilities. The society still begs for investments to provide an endowment to fund future experimental projects, but it now runs as a self-sustaining organisation, earning its own way. It was, I am sure, the right way to go. The RSA will always, however, face the dilemma that I encountered at Windsor: the need to make sure that the commercial imperatives do not contaminate the real purpose of the organisation.

This dilemma at Windsor and the RSA highlighted another issue, one that has continued to puzzle and concern me ever since. Charities are required by law to have a clear, stated, social purpose. This is not so of a business, which, in law, has obligations only to its owners, with a nod to the other stakeholders. Is this as it should be or should a business also have a clear social purpose? This is required under the constitution of Germany, one drawn up after the last war under the supervision of the occupying powers who, of course, included both Britain and America.

This was to be one of the big social and ethical questions we debated at our Windsor gatherings. These gatherings, or 'consultations' as we called them, were groups of twenty to thirty influential individuals from different parts of society. It was our task as the organisers to define the social and ethical issues that, in our view, needed debate. We then had to find those who could best contribute to the discussions and who might be encouraged to look anew at their own spheres of responsibilities. It should, desirably, be a mix of influential thinkers and heads of institutions across society. The discussions were private. We believed that people in senior roles learn best by listening to others whom they respect and by being forced to articulate their own views and principles. They don't appreciate being lectured or preached at. It was a very different form of education from the one I had presided over at the London Business School. I found it stimulating, although one never knew whether any minds or hearts were changed by the process. As I watched the participants drive out of the castle in their smart cars I would wonder whether it had all been anything more than an interesting weekend. Like all educational ventures, it was hard to know what the ultimate outcome would be.

There was one notable exception. A year after I had left Windsor I was asked out to lunch at the Institute of Directors. My host was the chairman of a well-known family business. 'You may wonder,' he said, 'why I wanted to see you. Well, this is a momentous day. Two years ago I attended one of those weekends at Windsor Castle. We talked about the great privileges and responsibilities of ownership. I went away wondering whether it was right that I should keep all those privileges to myself. Would it not be beneficial to us all if I shared both the privileges and the responsibilities with the people in the company? It took me two years to sort out the legal problems, but this day I have signed over half the company to the workers.'

Sometimes, I reflected, seeds do germinate if the soil is ready for them. I could only hope that other seeds had done the same, even though I never saw the results. Every teacher must feel the same.

In my role as warden I took a personal responsibility for organising a long-running series of consultations on 'The Future of Work'. This was in 1978, long before the topic became fashionable, but we tried hard, in our small team at Windsor, to focus on the issues that were on the far horizon. I still recall one of our early discussions when I first suggested that the term 'house husband' would one day be commonplace. The very idea, they all felt, was absurd. So much have times changed that, in some professional circles, it is now almost a badge of pride to be the man who stays at home.

Life was hard in Britain that year. Businesses were shedding labour. Unemployment was rising. The unions were flexing their muscles. It seemed clear to me that the days of the fully integrated company were coming to an end. No longer would businesses be able to offer full-time work for life to their employees. No longer would they seek to keep all the services they needed in-house. The term 'outsourcing' was not yet in vogue, but people were already beginning to subcontract the bits of their business that weren't critical. I foresaw some dangers – organisations could mistakenly subcontract the wrong bits, or put themselves at the mercy of their subcontractors – but I was interested in what this new trend would mean for the individual. It seemed clear that new sorts of work patterns were going to emerge, new types of career, new ways of organising one's life.

It was then that I came up with the metaphor of a 'portfolio life'. The idea was that more and more people would be driven, or might choose, to become independent workers, putting together a packet of different jobs, clients and types of work. 'It won't catch on,' I was told. But it has. The official statistics don't match the anecdotal evidence, largely because the existing statistical categories miss out many of these people. Some are straightforwardly self-employed, but many independents incorporate themselves as a business, in which case they are counted as full-time workers. There are currently nearly three million businesses in Britain with no employees, just the owner. Add to these the two million people who work for tiny organisations with fewer than five employees. Others work part time for one employer but do other work on the side. They are listed, however, as permanent part-time employees. Some others call themselves retired, a word that nowadays often describes a motley portfolio of activities, some of them remunerated, not all of which are declared. Added to these, there are, in Britain, ten million people of working age who are defined as economically inactive, most of them women. That does not mean that they are not working, as any housewife or mother will confirm. They may even be doing a bit of cash work on the side. They are unlisted portfolio workers.

This is what I now call the 'flea economy', tiny businesses and free agents of one sort or another, all adding value. They don't fit neatly into the current definitions of work, which are still based on the old industrial world. We are now in the knowledge and information world, where those tiny businesses or lone individuals can operate effectively and usefully. If I add together all those whom I would call fleas, many of them portfolio workers, it amounts to more than half the registered UK workforce. The world of work is much more fragmented than it seems from the official statistics. We need to warn those who are starting out that the world their parents experienced, one for which they have been prepared in their turn, will no longer be there for many, or, if it is, that it won't last for all of their working lives.

'Women have always been portfolio workers,' my wife reminded me, 'none of this is really new. It's just that you men have finally woken up to the way life is.' Not all of us, however, will find it that easy. Fully fledged portfolios are well suited to the middle-aged professional or manager who, with a mortgage paid off, perhaps some redundancy money tucked away or the promise of a deferred pension, can afford to take some risks and launch out on an independent life. In fact the idea first occurred to me when I spent a day at a pre-retirement course for IBM executives. The executives were worried about what to call themselves. 'Ex-IBMer' didn't sound too good. I suggested, half face-tiously, that since they would be putting together a varied collection of activities, they were really assembling a work portfolio, so why not call themselves 'Portfolio People'? The term seemed to grab their interest so I went on using it.

Later, during the Windsor discussions, we broadened the portfolio idea to include all the different varieties of work that people undertake. They included what we called 'waged work' and 'fee work', both forms of paid work, although independents typically charge fees in place of salaries or wages. The distinction is important. A fee is money paid for work done, a salary or wage is for time spent. The fee is calculated and proposed by the worker, the wage by the employer. There was also 'gift work', volunteer work of one sort or another, 'study work', with more and more mature students finding that study was indeed serious work, and, finally, 'home work', the uncounted, unpaid work involved in looking after the house or caring for relatives.

A sensible portfolio would contain elements of all four types of work, although the precise mix would change over time, depending on circumstances or priorities. I once met a young woman who, in response to the inevitable question 'What do you do?' replied, 'I write television plays.'

'Fantastic,' I said, impressed, 'would I have seen any of them?'

'Oh, they never get produced.'

'How sad. But what do you do for money then?'

'I pack eggs on Sunday,' she replied, 'boring and unsocial but it pays the bills.'

Since then, 'packing eggs' has become shorthand in our house for boring but lucrative work. Small bits of prostitution may be necessary, I tell myself, to pay for more virtuous activities. It is just one way of arranging the portfolio.

'Work-life balance' is, in my view, a misleading expression because it implies that work and life are two different things. Portfolio thinking holds that most of life is work, some of it boring, some lucrative, some worthwhile in its own right. It is the 'work balance' that matters. Even those in full employment need to consider the balance of their portfolio. To try to get that balance in one package from one job will always be difficult, but not impossible if the employer understands. And, yes, we do need to rest and refresh ourselves, but many find that a change is literally as good as a rest, that switching from one type of work to another is refreshing in itself. When I am writing in the country I plan the days to mix the actual writing (paid work) with periods of reading and research (study work) and some decent home work: shopping and cooking the evening meal. It's all work, but the mix of different types makes it pleasurable – for me, at least, and at my stage of life. I am also careful to allow a little time for R & R – the post-prandial snooze and some gentle tennis and walking. In truth, we are all portfolio workers, even though the balance of the portfolio will differ from one person to another and from one year to the next.

The more I thought about it the more I became enamoured of the possibilities of the independent portfolio life. I saw it as a sort of freedom, imprisoned as I was myself in an all day, all week job. People should be free, as I saw it, to arrange their lives to suit themselves, particularly when they reached middle age. Indeed, I argued and still believe that as we get older we should move out of organisations and leave more of the dwindling supply of those sort of jobs to the up and coming generations. To put it another way, in midlife most of us begin to lose some of our energy and enthusiasm for the daily grind. We hope, perhaps optimistically, that our diminishing energy is replaced by increased wisdom. But wisdom is needed in smaller bites. 'We value your experience and wisdom, John, and want to keep you around,' a friend's boss told him, 'but only on Tuesdays.' We ought, by the age of fifty, to be able to look after ourselves for at least the other six days.

Easy to say, while one is safe inside the organisation, imprisoning though it might be. I had not fully anticipated the downsides. After I wrote a book advocating the portfolio life I got a number of letters effectively saying, 'I took your advice, left my organisation to live a portfolio life, but my portfolio is still empty. What do you suggest that I do?' I had no good answer. Indeed, I myself was then nearing fifty and was uncomfortably aware that I might soon have to take my own medicine if my theories about the future were to be credible.

Chapter Ten
St Michael and St George

'What should I wear, and where would you like me to sit?' I was addressing the head verger of the great Chapel of St George that formed one side of the courtyard that housed our study centre and was key to a lot of its work. The duty canon had been called away and would not be able to preach the Sunday morning sermon. He had asked me to stand in for him. The verger was not impressed. 'You must wear what you please,' he said, 'and sit where you like. There is no precedent. No layman has ever preached here in the long history of this chapel.' I have no idea whether he was right or not, but it was a touch daunting to be breaking a centuries-old tradition. It had better be good. Unfortunately, just after I started my little sermon the sound system failed. I continued as best I could but I could not help but think that a human hand had been involved, careful lest the ears of the faithful be harmed by my irreverent thoughts.

Later that day he came up to me to apologise for 'the unfortunate malfunctioning of the sound system'. 'A pity,' he added, 'for they tell me that it was good, what you said.' I was mollified. I wondered, however, whether my father might not have agreed with the verger at the impropriety of my interpreting the word of God. Some years before I had preached at a weekday service for business people in Coventry Cathedral. My father, then, was not impressed. I was not qualified, he told me. I hoped, however, that he might now be pleasantly surprised to see where I had ended up, largely as a result of his death. So it was that my thoughts, that afternoon in the shadow of St George, went back to another beautiful church, this one in the fields of rural Ireland.

29 September, I remembered, was always a special day in my family. It was the feast day of St Michael, to whom my father's church was dedicated. The church was, to be strictly accurate, dedicated to St Michael and All Angels, which seemed to me, as a small boy, to be just a bit greedy, bagging so many for one small church. My parents made a big thing out of this patronal festival. My father would always find a high-profile cleric to preach at a special afternoon service and my mother would lay on a garden party for upwards of a hundred invited people, many of whom would have come down from Dublin for the afternoon. They were more leisured times back then, and the Church and its doings were still central to the life of the Protestant community in Southern Ireland.

The church was, and is, quite unlike any other village church. For one thing it is not in the village but set on a slight hill two miles away, from where it can be seen from the house of the man who built it at the end of the nineteenth century. Thomas Cooke Trench had been in Italy and he decided to create a small pure Romanesque church, modelled, it was said, on a chapel he had seen near Lake Garda. The marble walls were left unornamented. No inscriptions or plaques were permitted. This was a house of God, not of dead humans. I loved to be in it alone. The last thing I would do as a young boy before going back to my dreaded boarding schools would be to go there for a few minutes to say goodbye. Not many religious buildings lift one's spirits or give one peace. This one did.

It was a rare thing to find in the Irish countryside and was, perhaps, the main reason why my father never left that parish. The great challenge of his working life had been to rebuild a large part of the church after it was set on fire by a couple of frustrated burglars who had found nothing worth stealing. Once it was restored, I sensed that he was never going to leave it again, and he is now buried outside the vestry door he entered each morning for forty years.

The church was two hundred yards from our house, the vicarage, and it was the centre of our life during my boyhood. Sundays were special – we dressed up, not down, for the occasion, while Christmas and Easter were the climaxes of our year. Until I was eighteen or so I never queried any of this. It was part of the pattern of our lives and I did not enquire too deeply into the thinking behind it. I am left with a deep appreciation of holy places, so long as they are uncluttered and, preferably, empty. As for the religion that inspired their construction, that's another story.

Fast-forward some forty years from my boyhood and I find myself living beside that other beautiful holy place, the Chapel of St George in Windsor Castle. This one, however, is richly adorned with emblems of humanity's pride and glory. Monarchs are buried there with their tombs and chapels to remind us of who they were. Great banners hang above the choir with the insignia of the knights of the garter, nowadays elderly ex-prime ministers, dukes or royals in place of the young warriors of old. It is a place full of mankind's glories. At first sight God does not get a look in.

But I had a key, and late at night it was a different place. The tall slender columns of the nave, built in the English Perpendicular style, really did seem to reach up towards heaven. I would stand in the stillness and sense my insignificance and yet, somehow, be reconciled to it. In the six hundred years that had passed since this building had been started, many who thought themselves important had said their prayers here and yet, now, all that we have of them are the stones that cover their bones. Dust to dust indeed. But that need not be a reason for depression. Death is a useful deadline, a reminder that life is our brief opportunity to create something that might outlast us, as did the best of those who lie buried there. The craftsmen who first began work on this building knew that they would never see it finished, but they nevertheless made sure that it would be good and would last well beyond their deaths. It was a message that I used to impress on the directors of the companies as I showed them round the chapel late in the night. How far into the future did they look? How did they ensure that it was good? And what did that mean in their context?

I loved the chapel, full or empty, and the music. The male voice choir with its young choristers, one of them our son, was one of the best in England and sang Evensong six days a week with three services on Sundays. To me the services were more than a sacred choral concert; they were my space for meditation. While the choir sang and the canons read the scriptures and the prayers, I went into a private place in my head. Most of the time I did not pay attention to what was going on around me, but I felt that it was in some way good. I also relished the short communion services that took place every morning in one of the small sub-chapels. Anyone could attend but usually it was only the Dean, three canons and myself. For twenty minutes I lost myself in what was really a medieval ritual. In that setting it seemed usefully symbolic to be passing bread and wine between my colleagues. A good start to the day, before the trivialities of everyday work absorbed us.

I must have seemed very religious. My mother-in-law, coming to stay soon after we moved to Windsor, remarked in astonishment, 'What's happening? You've been to church three times today, and it's only Thursday!' The truth is that I was, and am, a cultural Christian. I am addicted to the grand old churches and cathedrals of England, to much of the music that has been composed to be played and sung in them, to many of their rituals and to their seventeenth-century language. I don't, however, have much time for the organisations that lie behind these structures. Like all organisations they often seem more interested in their own survival than in pursuing the real reason for their existence. That is not necessarily the fault of those who work in them, many of whom are dedicated people who give their lives to serve their god and their fellow beings. Organisations may be necessary but too many of them can be prisons and their warders more concerned with their own welfare than that of those in their care.

I watched and listened at my parents' table as visiting clerics discussed with my father, the archdeacon, the merits of different candidates for this bishopric or that deanship, while they railed against the central office for the imposition of yet more paperwork and lobbied, ever so subtly – 'I feel I am called' was the way they put it – for this or that posting where their talents, they believed, would be better employed, and where, I often cynically noted, the housing and schools were better. It wasn't, I reflected, that different from Shell or any of the other organisations I had encountered in the business world. Rules, regulations and hierarchy were their bones and arteries, relationships, and the politics they engendered, their blood.

Does faith require all this organisational paraphernalia to be effective, I asked myself? Jesus, the founder of much of this, did not think so. Organisations, however, seldom commit suicide and these ones had been going for a very long time, surviving internal revolutions, breakaways and reformations. They weren't about to go away.

It was easy to be cynical about the organisations of religion. More worrying for me was the growing realisation that I could not go along with much of their teaching. Surely I could not be expected to believe that there was some man up there – or was it a woman? – designing and organising the world, nor that his son was somehow watching over me and, as we used to pray, preventing me in all my doings. (It was many years before I realised that 'prevent' was old English for 'go before'.) Did they really believe in the resurrection of the body, and in places like heaven and hell? Personally, I would prefer everlasting death to everlasting life and I take comfort from thinking that the complex molecules that make up my physical body will in due course decompose and eventually turn into something else, maybe a tree, maybe a frog, who knows? Perhaps this is my true immortality.

Which is why I want my body to be buried not burnt – to ease the transformation.

We should, I feel, take the Christian myths seriously but not literally, any more than the Greeks took their myths as fact. We have to remember that the Bible was not always one big book, that even the bits that were eventually written down were not going to be read by many. Until the invention of printing the great majority of people never saw a book. When they did, it was often in a language, Latin, they could not understand. Instead they listened to stories in their churches and chapels and looked at the paintings in front of them on the walls. Anyone who has had to speak to large groups of people knows that, to hold their attention, you are well advised to tell stories to illustrate your point and, wherever possible, to show pictures because most of us remember images more easily than concepts. Jesus himself knew that. He told stories that related to the lives of his listeners that conjured up images that were later to be displayed on those church walls.

Stories don't have to be literally true to carry important messages and truths. I have myself invented or altered stories better to convey a message. To illustrate the concept of the 'second curve' I used to tell a story about losing my way in the hills behind Dublin. An Irishman beside the road gave me directions. 'Go straight on as you are heading,' he said, 'and on down the valley. After a mile or so you'll cross a bridge and you'll see Davy's Bar on the other side. You can't miss it. Have you got that?'

'Yes,' I replied.

'Well then, half a mile before you get there, turn right up the hill.' Too many people, I would tell audiences, find themselves at Davy's Bar in life, too late by then to retrace their steps to the road they should have taken.

Many people have asked me for directions to Davy's Bar. There is no such place. My story had a basis in fact but I embellished it to make it memorable in the hope that people would also remember the point behind the story. Without meaning to be sacrilegious, I believe that many of the Bible stories are like Davy's Bar – memorable stories exaggerated to convey an important truth. They are not meant to be taken literally.

Stories offer what I term 'low definition' concepts. They don't tell you precisely what to do. They offer clues to a misty idea. If, moreover, they are part of an oral not a written tradition you can't trade quotations back and forth as religious fundamentalists like to do. Memory tricks us all, one person's version of what was said will differ from another, even from a participant in the same conversation. It is, I decided, silly to take literally stories that were not written down until decades after the event. I was much impressed the first time I came across Samuel Butler's satire on Victorian society and religion, *Erewhon*, in which he casts himself as a visitor in some imaginary land, and even more taken by the sequel, *Erewhon Revisited*, his account of his return visit many years later, when he learns of the stories that had grown up around his earlier visit – how, for instance, his escape from the island in a hot-air balloon had been magnified over time into a version of the Ascension.

None of which should diminish the importance of the Bible stories, or indeed of similar mythic stories in other religions. They point to important truths. The Bible itself is a work of great human wisdom from which we have much to learn if we work at its interpretation. My favourite religious painting was originally commissioned for the council chamber in the town hall of San Sepolcro, a village in the north-east corner of Tuscany towards the end of the fifteenth century. It is a painting of the Resurrection by Piero della Francesca. The mural dominates the room in what is now a museum and must, at the time, have had a powerful effect on the council when it sat there. Christ is depicted literally stepping out of a stone coffin while Roman soldiers lie asleep beside it. The event is set in a Tuscan landscape, the kind of scenery that would be familiar to all those looking at it. This was not something happening in a faraway land, the artist was implying, but right here, where they lived.

The Christ in this painting is a formidable figure. Not particularly kindly, not smiling, his eyes follow you wherever you stand. He seems to be directing himself to you. What's it all about? Down the years I have looked at this picture too many times to count, standing, often alone, in that room. To me he seems to be saying, 'If I can survive all this and get up and live again, then so can you.' We, each of us, die a lot of little deaths in the course of our lives, I reflect. But none of them should deter us from starting again, or from using that new start to make amends for anything we did in the past. 'Be brave, begin now on your new life,' this figure says to me. This, of course, is my own interpretation, but it means more to me than some woolly idea of a new life in some imagined heaven. At least I can do something about it.

I once had the idea of producing a book offering my interpretation of some of the more well-known Biblical stories. Instead, as my Windsor time was coming to an end, I was approached by Robert Foxcroft who was then the producer of 'Thought for the Day' on the Today programme on BBC radio. He asked me to try my hand at some 'Thoughts'. These were two-minute forty-five-second religious reflections on the events of the day. Known colloquially as the 'God slot', they were the BBC's bow to its obligation to include a proportion of religion, of every kind, in its broadcasts. We weren't popular, we speakers, with the presenters. At peak time we had what no one else was allowed, almost three minutes of uninterrupted chat, on a topic of our choice. Yes, we had to check our script the night before with the Religious Affairs Department of the BBC, but our minders didn't pass on any details to the presenters who had to sit there not knowing what was coming, listen and never, ever, ask any questions.

You could always tell if the presenters thought you were worthy of that special three minutes by the tone of voice in which they introduced you. I did the 'Thought' on and off for twenty years and gradually, I think and hope, earned the respect of those distinguished men and women whose voices provide the background to the breakfasts of four or five million middle-class Britons. Brian Redgrave was in charge for my first appearance. I remember my delight when he chuckled aloud at the end of my piece. So he actually listened! Such little things can make our day.

My wife gave me two pieces of advice when I started: 'Don't preach and never use God as the subject of a sentence. It puts people off and, anyway, how do you know what God thinks?' It was a wise warning. I used, instead, what I called 'implicit theology'. I argued that Christianity was based on the doctrine of incarnation, or God in us. That left open the question of what God is. I regarded him/it as our basic instinct for good, our conscience, our altruistic gene. The neuroscientist Antonio Damasio makes a stab at defining spirituality in a naturalistic way that accords with my sense of what you might call Godness. 'I assimilate the notion of [the] spiritual to an intensive experience of harmony,' he explains, 'to the sense that the organism is functioning with the greatest possible perfection. The experience unfolds with the desire to act towards others with kindness and generosity.'

John Donne captures the idea of harmony more poetically, writing of 'dwelling in that house where there shall be no darkness nor dazzling, but one equal light; no noise nor silence, but one equal music; no fears nor hopes, but one equal possession; no ends nor beginnings, but one equal eternity . . .' For Donne it is faith in God that leads one to this *desideratum*. I can share his dream but see no need for the help of his God to bring it about. There can be too much upward delegation in religion. Nonetheless, if you don't believe that there is some source of goodness in the world there can be no right or wrong, no correction to pure selfishness.

I am, I suppose, a sort of Christian humanist, although fortunately I have never been asked to define my beliefs. If all that essence of goodness that some call God is truly part of us, I argued, then we should not need to use religious language to get the message across. The language of everyday life should suffice, and the message of Christianity could be found in the stories of our own lives if you looked for it, just as it was there in the parables in the Bible. As Tolstoy put it, 'God is life', you find him or it in the very process of living. I saw it as my role to try to unearth the meaning of things in the everyday events of the world.

They were tricky things to do, those 'Thoughts'. You were required to reflect on some item in the news or which might be touched on in the programme that morning. It helped if you could tell a personal anecdote and introduce a bit of humour and, importantly, a moral to the story. And all in 450 words. Ideally, it should leave people with something to think about as they went to work that morning.

Just to make it more challenging, there might be, as Robert Foxcroft pointed out, four or five million people tuned in but that didn't mean that they were listening. For many of them 'Thought for the Day' was an alarm clock, reminding them to get up, to get out of the house, to put the eggs on, whatever. You had some ten seconds at the beginning to say something to attract their attention. Oh, and it was live radio – no pre-recordings allowed, in case news was breaking that needed a reflection. So no stutterings, slurrings or mistakes. It had to be right first time.

It was a challenge. I used to reserve the whole of the preceding day to prepare my 450 words because there was no guarantee that I would get it right the first time. I was paid twenty-seven pounds per minute, which is not a bad rate, but since there were fewer than three of those minutes this was not a recipe for wealth creation. However, on the principle that those who teach learn most, I learnt a lot about my beliefs during those twenty years. Trying to make sense of the odd things that go on in the world and in our lives is a practical way of doing philosophy.

One morning the studio rang me at 5.30 a.m. Drowsily, I answered. It was thirty minutes too early, I said. Yes, they replied, but there had been an earthquake in San Francisco in the night. The lines were all down. No one knew how bad it was. I must dump my prepared piece and provide a moral message in two hours' time. Was this a cue, I wondered, for a reflection on God's mysterious ways, on the puzzle of how a good God could let this sort of thing happen? Not my style, I thought. You can't make sense of that sort of event, but you can reflect on how one should respond to it. I focused on two of our friends there whom we were, as it happened, due to visit in a month's time. I wondered aloud on the air how they were faring, if they were still alive, whether we would ever again go up to the wine country together. I pondered, then, how we can, in general, best help those in distress. By showing that we cared, I said. And you don't do that by holding back in case you invade their privacy. 'So call your friends in America as soon as the phones are working. It will help them, it will help you. Try now, before you leave home.' It wasn't what you might call religious, just common sense, but someone needed to say it that morning, while the newscasters recited the horrors of what could have happened and individuals buried in rubble became just statistics.

When well done, those 'Thoughts' did provide that short pause for reflection amid the often wearisome succession of political interviews and depressing newsbites. It is those pauses for reflection that we all need and for which religion can provide a structure. I once suggested to the *Today* team that, instead of a spoken 'Thought', they should have a 'Pause for Thought', two minutes of reflective silence. They told me it was clear I did not understand radio. Silence was anathema. I liked the idea, though. The nation, or a large chunk of it, reflecting together every morning.

Call it prayer, or worship or meditation, it is a way to draw back from the busyness of life and ponder the whys of it all. My father did it every morning, saying Matins by himself in his church up the road. I have friends who regularly meditate for twenty minutes or an hour every morning. My wife and I walk on the heath opposite our home for forty minutes before breakfast. We plan the day ahead together but most of the time we just walk, in comfortable silence. Were there a beautiful church or chapel nearby I might go there, but nature is a chapel in itself, ever-changing, always there, always free.

Art, I find, also takes me out of my immediate world into another place, encouraging me to look at things differently. On a visit to a gallery with our children and their partners we have, on occasion, suggested that we should each choose two of the exhibits that especially speak to us, buy the postcards of them in the gallery shop and then, over a meal, describe what thoughts they arouse in us. Theatre, too, at its best, puts you into an unfamiliar situation, forcing you to contemplate dilemmas and quandaries that may have echoes in your own life but which you can view more objectively when they are a few rows of seats away from you. Great theatre is terrifying sometimes, confronting you with issues you would rather shun but know you shouldn't. Galleries and theatres are my secular chapels. In their different ways they help me to ponder what Lucretius called 'rerum natura', the nature of things.

My form of faith relies on my working things out for myself, what I believe about the purpose of life, about morality and what happens afterwards. It isn't easy. It can lead to what Pope Benedict XVI regards as the prevailing danger of our age, secular relativism, or a pick-and-mix Christianity where we each decide for ourselves what bits we like and we want to call right and wrong. It is not a new problem. There is a verse in the Book of Judges in the Bible that says, 'In those days there was no king in Israel, but every man did what was right in his own eyes.'

The Pope believes that people need moral guidelines, based on a faith in God. I can see that it does make it easier to separate right from wrong if you can buy into the faith. I have also observed that many intellectuals convert to Roman Catholicism as they get nearer to death. It solves all those intellectual dilemmas. There is comfort there if you can buy into the premise. I witnessed, however, back in my native Ireland, the dangers of the moral dictatorship that can come from the required obedience to the certainties of that religion. People ceased to think for themselves back then; the rules were precise and the local priest the arbiter of all that they did. It was a religion of fear, not of joy, with consequences spelt out for those who erred. Confession was, as I saw it, a way for the priesthood to keep control of the local population. Imagine how convenient it would be for a business if everyone felt obliged to reveal all their misdeeds and malevolent thoughts to their manager every week, with penances required for every misdemeanour. Such a system would drain initiative and energy from individuals who would find it simpler to leave it to their seniors to tell them what to do. I am sure that many of the priests were godly men and benevolent in intention, but they were part of an authoritarian system that recognised no doubt and accepted no criticism, one that could not even accept that there might be anything wrong or rotten in their own regime, as there later turned out to be. As a result Ireland, when I lived there, was a guilt-ridden and repressed nation, not surely the way their God would have wanted it.

Ireland is different now. The Irish have embraced secular relativism with an excess of enthusiasm. Other nations have followed suit. John Paul II was a charismatic and an undoubtedly holy man, but that did not make his social teaching any more attractive or, in my view, always relevant to the needs of the world. People in the Western world distinguished between the man and his teachings so that, paradoxically, the authority of the Church was weakened during his papacy once they realised that they could have the man without the doctrine. By extension that meant they could have God without the commandments, spirituality without any inconvenient moral imperatives. Once the rules are ignored you are left with licence – to do what you please.

The new permissiveness is the problem that religion faces everywhere, not just in the Catholic Church but throughout the Protestant community and Islam, too. With the commandments ignored or God denied, you have to learn how to work out your own beliefs and code of conduct. Unsurprisingly, most people find this difficult. In this increasingly secular world a new role for the churches, I believe, would be to become vehicles for philosophical education, teaching us how to think, not how to behave. They probably have neither the skills nor the credibility to do this, which leaves our civilisation with a dangerous gap.

We don't want governments moving into the gap and taking on the role of moral authority in an age without religion. There are already signs of this happening. Laws pop up every day laying down rules for looking after our children, for respecting our neighbours, avoiding damage to the environment, taking care of our health and lifestyles. Soon they will take on the responsibility for finding us suitable work, homes and appropriate education. That is the path that communism trod when religions were outlawed and no one dared risk letting people think for themselves. Relativism is indeed a very present danger, but it has to be dealt with, not by reinforcing the rules, nor by unquestioning faith in some higher order, but by better education, one that equips people to think for themselves.

That might be called the task of philosophy, and philosophy of a sort that I was beginning to see as my calling. After my father's funeral I had thought that religion might provide me with the certainty that I had envied in him and the sense of purpose in life. Windsor was my apprenticeship. During my four years there I listened to over one hundred different theologians of various faiths. I met most of the then bishops of the Church of England who came to St George's House to gain some overview of the wider world beyond the parishes where they had spent much of their ministry. Twice a year, twenty up-and-coming parish priests came to us for a month on a sort of refresher course. I got to know them well. I met good men, all still men at that time, dedicated, mostly, to their work and believing most, if not all, of the creeds we professed in the chapel. It was education by immersion and I learnt a lot. But I also realised that I could not believe what they believed.

The Christian story was important, I was sure. Its messages needed to be interpreted and translated for our time and place and for the work we nowadays do. That was what I felt I needed to do, mindful always that the translation needed to be accessible and interesting to the modern Gentiles, those outside the traditional faiths. Towards the end of my four years in Windsor, the Dean asked me if I would like to be ordained. This time around I had no hesitation in saying, 'I appreciate the suggestion but no, it's not for me.'

Chapter Eleven
A Portfolio Life

He sidled up to me as people were gathering for my farewell party at Windsor in July 1981.

'I have just one piece of advice for you,' Bill said. 'Make sure that you have something to do when you get out of bed each morning. Retirement can kill you otherwise.' He meant it well. He and his business had been one of the best customers of our centre and he knew whereof he spoke, having watched too many friends die too early. But I was taken aback. He thought that I was retiring. I was forty-nine and nothing was further from my thoughts. Twenty-five years later I still think it a bad idea.

I had, however, made a tactical mistake. I had tentatively offered to leave my post as warden of St George's House after four years instead of five, to allow my planned successor to take over early, and had been rather affronted and annoyed to have my offer promptly accepted. I am, I confess, addicted to a sort of false modesty, putting myself down in the hope that my listener will pull me up. I had hoped that the Dean, to whom I had offered my resignation, would come back to me saying, 'Thank you for offering, but you are far too valuable for us to let you go before you have to.' Instead he seemed only too happy to get rid of me. Two more lessons from life – don't offer something you don't really mean, and don't fish for compliments or reassurance. They may not come.

Suddenly, I had to contemplate living the kind of free-agent life that

I had been forecasting in our Windsor discussions, even recommending, in fact, for people over fifty. 'Get out of the way,' I remembered that I had said, 'and leave organisations to the young and energetic. We are not as indispensable as we like to think we are. Most of us cling on too long, hoping that our wisdom more than compensates for our failing energies.' Now I was skewered by my own words.

It was an inconvenient time. It always is. I had decided that social philosophy would be my new calling, but, like St Augustine, not quite yet. Most of us have to be pushed into the portfolio life. We had two teenage children still at school in Windsor. I had a small part-time teaching contract back at the London Business School but otherwise had no visible means of support. Elizabeth was startled, to put it mildly, when I told her what I had, unintentionally, done and confronted her with the fact that we would be leaving in three months' time to go back to our London pad, which was currently and lucratively rented out. Magnificently, she looked at the positive side. 'Now you can really concentrate on your writing,' she said.

My literary agent was not so sure. He came to lunch. 'Don't give up your day job,' he said.

'I have just done exactly that,' I replied.

'Oh dear.'

'But I've got a couple of ideas.'

'It's not a good time for new books. Your textbook is doing quite well, why don't you update it?'

'No, I want to write for a wider public, to alert them to what is happening in our society.'

He wasn't happy. The thought that he might become responsible for propping up my future life did not excite him. My ideas on the future of our society did not appeal to him, nor, he suspected to any future publisher. He begged me to get another job.

'No,' I said, firmly, 'I am going portfolio.'

'What's that in English?'

April 1930 Joan Scott married Brian Handy, the curate of her local church in Bray, Ireland. That ⟨sta⟩rted a chain of events that is still unwinding.

⟨In t⟩he beginning was a baby – myself in my ⟨fath⟩er's arms.

Then the scrubbed-up schoolboy – with my younger sisters.

I longed to be a sportsman, but the House Rugby team was the farthest I got (I am bottom right).

Life is getting serious – I am now nineteen and at Oxford.

But not that serious – at the Oriel College Ball with Catherine Christie.

last appearance on a football pitch – at the Selangor Club in Kuala Lumpur.

other things were on my mind – myself Elizabeth.

And, back in London, we made it official.

Now the chain starts again – with Kate, our first-born.

I probably missed the catch – w
Scott, our son.

All together now, even the dog is in the family.
Photograph by Elizabeth Handy.

Posing in Windsor Castle – as
Warden of St George's House.

early not one of my more
eting addresses – as
airman of the Royal
ciety of Arts in 1988.

anyone listening out there? – broadcasting on the BBC.
otograph by Elizabeth Handy.

Not all mine, alas, only a corner of it – in fr[ont]
of our Tuscan hamlet. *Photograph by Elizab[eth]
Handy.*

But the view from our window was
spectacular – with Kate, our daughter.

And San Gimiganano was just down the r[oad]
– with Elizabeth and Scott.

woman of many parts – Elizabeth in her kitchen in London. *Photograph by Elizabeth Handy.*

Impertinently teaching teachers – as President of the North of England Conference.

Edgy stuff this publicity business – promoting my book *The Elephant and the Flea*. Photograph by Elizabeth Handy.

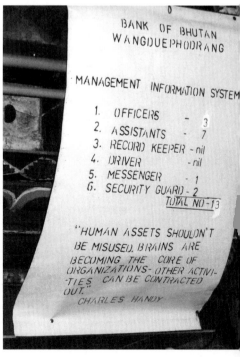

But it gets my message into the oddest pla – poster in the window of the bank.

'I am going freelance, independent, putting together a basket of activities, centred around my writing.'

'Well,' he concluded, 'don't count on that to provide your bread and butter. Of all my hundred or so authors only two or three make more than ten thousand pounds a year from their books.'

He departed, slumped in gloom. The mood was infectious. The prospect of freedom was no longer so enticing. Building a portfolio, I was about to discover, was harder in practice than in theory, particularly if it was one's first attempt. All my life I had really been reacting to what needed to be done, to the telephone or the in tray in one form or another, taking initiatives here and there but with my life essentially driven by what came in and what was expected of me. Suddenly, nothing came into that in tray, only the newspaper. There were no meetings to go to, no calls to return, no appointments to keep, no targets, no appraisals. The diary was empty. Bliss, I had thought it would be, but it wasn't. More like panic. I no longer underestimated the difficulties of moving from a sheltered prison to the open world. I felt as if I had stepped out of a nice little cave in my life, which might have been uncomfortable and claustrophobic but was at least a place of safety, into a void, with no idea of how far down it was or what the bottom would be like when I landed.

More disturbing still was the loss of a clear identity. Who was this new Charles Handy? A portfolio life described the way I lived but it said nothing about who I was or what I did. I was acutely aware that I had no label to tell people where I belonged or what I was qualified to do. 'How are you going to describe yourself?' a friend asked. 'You can't call yourself "the ex-warden" for too long.' The problem was brought home to me very shortly, when I started doing 'Thought for the Day' the month after I left Windsor. The presenters needed to introduce the speaker with a link to some organisation or profession so that the listeners could know where he or she was coming from, to put them in an identity box.

To begin with they did label me as the recent warden of St George's House, but that, as my friend had predicted, didn't last long. Then I was introduced as coming from the London Business School where I was still a visiting professor. This was such an unlikely source for a speaker on the God slot that I rather liked it. Later I was presented to the listeners as chairman of the Royal Society of Arts, which suggested a broader background. Finally, when all institutional connections had faded away, they introduced me as just Charles Handy. By then I was seeing it as a badge of my independence to appear on a list of conference participants as the only one without any institutional or professional label attached. At first, however, I had felt strangely naked. I clung on to my title of Professor. Professor Charles Handy gave me a form of professional clothing. 'Why?' asked Elizabeth. 'You don't profess any more, at least not officially. My name on its own has always been enough for me. Why do you men always want more to justify your existence?' Good question. Insecurity, I suppose.

This is your opportunity, Elizabeth reminded me, to explore other aspects of yourself. I had been living in a series of comfortable prisons: Shell, the business school, Windsor. They had all taught me something but they had also locked me into roles. In Windsor I was typically addressed as 'Warden' by everyone except close colleagues. Was this odd Victorian person me, I would wonder? I sometimes felt that I was just an actor in some bizarre play. In all my jobs, I realised now, I had needed to watch what I said in case it went against the interests of my organisation. I was always looking over my shoulder to see who might be listening. Freedom of speech may be a human right but it can be unwise to rely on it when your salary is paid by someone else. Now, as the unattached Charles Handy, the only person I could harm would be myself. I could say and write what I really believed, be who I wanted to be, go where the fancy took me, work only for those I valued. I saw myself as a social philosopher now, rather than any kind of management expert, although people in search of a label to pin on me often called me a consultant or, later, management guru, a title I grew to hate.

All the same, my agent was right. Few are those authors who can rely on their books to support them and their families, particularly if those books are non-fiction and unlikely to attract film rights or radio serialisation. I was amazed, and more than a little dismayed, to learn that over one hundred thousand new titles are published in Britain every year. There is not room enough in a bookstore to display them all, let alone keep them there for months on end. The average book disappears from most bookstore shelves after six months at most, and out of sight is too often out of mind. Thank goodness for Amazon, which still keeps the long tail of my past books in their huge warehouses. A visit one year to the Frankfurt Book Fair was even more depressing – twenty miles of books, only a tiny few of which were mine. Authors are, rightly, advised by their agents or publishers never to go near the place. I once asked my publisher what they found was the best way to keep a backlist alive. 'Get the author to write a new book,' was his response. There would, I could see, be no let-up if I were to embark on a serious career as an author.

Meantime I had to get some money coming in. It was very strange, after twenty-five years, to have no monthly salary, with tax already deducted, slipping into one's bank account. I had to generate an income, and soon, and remember, too, to put some of it away for the tax that would inevitably be required of me at some stage. Books wouldn't help in the immediate future. They take time to write and as long again for the publishers to get them into the shops. My first book, a textbook, *Understanding Organisations*, was selling well enough, but getting older. I had a new one on the go called *Gods of Management*, my first attempt at writing for the practising manager, but reviewers had not enthused. 'I hope that I will never have to work in any of Charles Handy's organisations,' said one, 'or live to see the world he describes.' I could not count on instant riches from it.

So it was that I became for a time a jobbing lecturer, giving seminars and talks on company training programmes. My two books accompanied me. They were my sales aids, the least obtrusive way of promoting myself and my ideas. A decorous way of advertising. All we independents have to do it but, like most people, I suppose, I hated having to sell myself or my wares. It seemed somehow indecent. Ideally, one should only have to respond to demands, but, I was uncomfortably aware, those demands have first to be stimulated. I now warn would-be portfolio workers that it can take up to seven years before the calls for one's work are self-sustaining.

It was all the fault of the culture I grew up in. A becoming modesty was urged on us. It made for a gentler society, everyone disclaiming any pretensions to success or talent. 'It's nothing really,' I can hear myself saying, or, 'I just write to keep myself out of trouble.' But if you don't shout how do people know you are there? Don't boast yourself is the answer, let other people do it for you if you must. Hire an agent, I was told. All independents have agents – look at actors, models, sport stars, pop and opera singers both, even writers. There are agents for plumbers and electricians and for temporary workers of all types, including managers. Manpower, the employment agency, has more people on its books than any organisation employs. In the flea economy that I see coming, indeed is already here, these agents are the intermediate employers, connecting talents and skills with customers, the job that organisations used to do. So, yes, I too had gone out and found myself a literary agent, but he didn't like boasting either, even for me. Three years after starting my portfolio life I collected all my scripts for 'Thought for the Day' and suggested to him that they might make a good little book.

'Oh, I don't think that anyone would be interested,' he said dismissively. I had some secret pleasure some years later when he, no longer my agent, just a friend, came to stay one weekend. I left the published book by his bedside. He had the grace to laugh.

But if my literary agent was averse to boasting, I knew someone who would. After three years of my portfolio existence, Elizabeth was in despair at my life. I was rushing hither and yon, speaking at business dinners, lecturing on company courses, writing the odd article but with no time for those big books that I had planned. I was exhausting myself, wasn't around the home much and, worst of all, was making very little money. The trouble was that in my previous existences I had done a lot of speaking at dinners and on courses for free, just because it was part of my job. I had not realised that you could charge money for these if you were independent. Elizabeth decided that she would have to take this in hand. To start with she rang up the last three places I had spoken at. 'I'm sorry,' she said, 'but the Professor forgot to send you the invoice for his fee. He suggests that he charges you x pounds plus expenses. Is this acceptable?' It always was, so she soon started to push the fees up. Finally, I had an agent who was not afraid to boast and who genuinely believed that I had something worth saying.

Nevertheless those first seven years of portfolio living were far from easy. I had three concerns at the top of my mind – first, and most pressing, was a roof over my head and some cash coming in, then the management of the physical and temporal spaces in our lives and, not least, the education of our teenage children. But none of these mattered, I realised, as much as the fundamental question of what my work was now going to be focused on. Freedom is fine, but freedom for what? is more difficult to answer. The freedom to live one's own life, I was discovering, meant more than setting ourselves up in business. It involved serious thought about our aims and priorities in life, even about how we could best arrange our physical space and allocate our time. Suddenly, I sensed, I was having to do philosophy for real, trying to work out what my life was all about, what mattered most and where or when I did it. How lucky I was in Shell, I reflected, where all these things were decided for me by my superiors – until the day came when I realised that I could not go along with their priorities. There are few things more uncomfortable in life than being used for purposes that are not yours by people you don't always respect.

Still, even if you don't necessarily respect them, those people are around. I had not anticipated how lonely life could be without colleagues. Projects are not such fun when there is no one to discuss them with. Success seems empty when there is nobody to celebrate with and failure doubly depressing with no one around to console you. Some new portfolio workers join loose partnerships of other independents, linking up with them when projects need extra skills. My sort of writing and mentoring was too idiosyncratic to need or attract anyone else. Others opt for shared spaces where at least they can have coffee together and complain about the taxman or their accountant. I could not afford to work anywhere except in my own home. In truth I could not afford much of anything at first. Did that matter? Not as much as I thought it would, because I was doing what I had chosen to do – creating word pictures, being a wordsmith, which sounds more romantic than sitting in front of a computer all morning, which was the reality. I had discovered an important truth, that if you care deeply about what you are doing then nothing else matters too much.

But despite all my grandiose philosophical musings, it was money that mattered most during those first years of independence. It always does, but particularly when it is hard to know or predict where it is going to come from and when. Being in charge of your life does not, I found, necessarily mean that you can control the most essential part of it, the finances. As long as I was employed, I came to realise, I had in effect sold all my time to the organisation. I had become a willing slave albeit a well-remunerated one. Having sold all my time in advance, more money for the same time would always be welcome as long as I could persuade them that I was worth it. More was always going to be better. Any bargaining was only about how much more and whether I deserved it. Now that I was employing myself, more money usually meant more time spent making it. The cost benefit calculation might now be different as an independent. More might not be better if it used up too much time, or if it meant doing what I disliked, was in the wrong place or, even, conceivably immoral.

Money is never the only criterion of success. That is not news. What is strange is the way so many people nevertheless act as if it was. For many it is a means to an end, the way to provide a better life for one's family, to pay for all the good things in life. That, however, can turn into a Faustian bargain, if they become trapped in doing what they come to hate because of what they need to have. Some, on the other hand, decide to be priests, nurses or artists, paid little for following their vocation. They may choose to work for almost nothing in a cause, like my aunt, a medical missionary, who gave her life to the poor of Bihar in India, living for twenty years in a whitewashed cell in a missionary compound and dying early, still passionately devoted to her Indian patients. Perhaps money is rightly called compensation, compensation for not having any other reason for doing what you do. Back home on leave, while I was still working for Shell and giving most of my attention to my leisure time, she could not conceive how I could be living what she saw as such a shallow life, dedicated largely to my own pleasure.

As I embarked on my portfolio life I was once again, I reflected, going back to my roots. When I was growing up in the Irish vicarage we lived, I thought, very comfortably and agreeably, but there was never any spare cash around. My father kept a tight eye on our finances and encouraged us to entrust any birthday or Christmas gifts to his home-made bank where he kept account cards for each of us, faithfully recording all monies out and in but where overdrafts were never on the agenda. My mother was given a weekly housekeeping allowance but was expected to produce a precise account of what she had spent at the end of the week.

She found this hugely onerous, never able to recall what she had spent on what. Looking over her shoulder one week I saw quite a large amount under the heading 'SPG'. Why, I asked her, when we had so little, was she giving so much to the Society for the Propagation of the Gospel, a well-known missionary society? 'Sssh,' she said, 'don't tell, but SPG stands for Something Probably Grub.' It was, I later heard, my sister Margaret's suggestion. I don't know if my father ever guessed, but if he did he never said a word.

One result of this cash-starved existence was my private resolution never to be poor, if I could help it. Mind you, my ambitions weren't that high. Back in the fifties I reckoned that two thousand pounds a year would do me fine, plus a Bentley Continental as an extra. That was five times the then starting salary at companies like Shell. Oil companies now pay starting salaries to graduates of around thirty thousand pounds so I suppose the equivalent today of my ambitions would be a hundred and fifty thousand pounds – not so modest after all. It was one reason why I decided to join Shell, only to discover eventually that the rewards were not worth what it would cost me in other ways.

Given my monetary ambitions at the beginning it was odd that I should find myself progressively reducing my salary over the years as I moved from the oil world to academia and then to work with the Church where my salary was actually below the official poverty level, and finally to the precarious state of self-employment. I had not, I realised, escaped as fully as I thought from the shades of the vicarage. My father was paid a stipend, not a salary. The distinction is important. A stipend is intended to be enough to sustain you so that you can get on with your calling. It is not intended to be a measure of your worth. The idea of doing something only, or even partly, for the money it paid would have been strange to my father. You should do what you feel you ought to do, he believed, irrespective of the pay and just hope that the money is enough, and if it isn't you should cut your cloth accordingly. Going out to make more of it would never have occurred to him. Hence the shortage of spare cash. He refused to borrow, too. An overdraft was almost as bad as adultery in his eyes and he was greatly distressed when I persuaded my, and not accidentally his, bank to allow me one in my student days.

To my surprise I had turned out more like him than I ever thought I would. But there was still the other part of me, the part that rejected the vicarage world, which liked spending money on the sort of things we didn't buy in my youth: restaurant meals, the theatre, taxis, flowers, wine – unnecessary things. It is then that I am uncomfortably reminded of Adam Smith, that wise Scotsman, who observed that while economic growth was obviously a good thing, in that it made life easier for everyone, too much of it for too long would result in a surfeit of all manner of unnecessary things. Looking at the shopping malls of our cities today I can't help feeling that he was right. But, I then ask myself, isn't that what money is for – to buy things that we hope will enrich our lives, even if some of them are not strictly necessary? Who are we, anyway, to tell people what is necessary and what just floss, cluttering up the streets and mucking up the environment with more unnecessary packaging? And don't all those unnecessary things provide employment to many, some of them in the Third World where, goodness knows, they need the jobs? Besides, VAT is loaded onto unnecessary things rather than the essentials like food, so the more unnecessary stuff that is sold the higher the tax revenue that pays for the other essentials that are funded by the state. Greed, envy and gluttony are not sins to the economist, but the essential foundations of prosperity.

It was another wise economist, Keynes, who said that it was only after we are all rich that we can 'once more value ends above means and prefer the good to the useful. But the time for this is not yet . . . Avarice and usury and precaution must be our gods for a little longer still. For they can lead us out of our tunnel of economic necessity into daylight.' But how rich did he think rich was? Browsing through the business section of any paper it is not unusual to learn that a few of our home-grown industrial barons had each taken home over four or five million pounds in pay in the past year. Some of them even get almost as much when they are sacked. And that's just Britain. In America they would make ten times as much. What do they do with it all, I wondered? Why do they need it? And is it fair that they should get so much more than the people who work with them? Or people like doctors and teachers and the police who do equally valuable work?

Those corporate chieftains will almost certainly never get around to spending all that money. They don't have the time and they may well not have the inclination to go out to buy houses, yachts or old paintings. It might, I sometimes think, be simpler to take out an advertisement in the papers saying how rich they are, or just circulate the *Sunday Times* Rich List to all their friends. Warren Buffet, the world's second richest man after Bill Gates, lives simply, spends little. His wealth is just a measure of his business acumen. 'It goes with the job,' such people say, 'I didn't seek it and I don't think about it.' If you are a doctor, success is measured in the patients you heal; if a teacher, in the students who learn and thrive; if you are in business, success is measured by the money you make. It's the way you keep the score.

They could give it away, and a growing number do. Some, like Buffet, wait until they die, when their foundations become their principal heirs. Others, like Bill Gates, can't wait for that sort of post-mortem philanthropy and do it, munificently, in their lifetime. A growing number of young multimillionaires are giving both money and time to causes that they have made their own. These new philanthropists want now to make a difference more than to make money. They already have more than enough and want to see that the surplus does something useful. Such people help to make big money respectable. They redeem some of the more blatant excesses of capitalism and may be setting a fashion. Already the 'rich lists' are balanced by the 'giving lists' in both Britain and America.

Most of us, however, don't have that choice. We do what we do and a little more money would be nice, thank you. 'It's the economy, stupid,' goes every politician's mantra, in the belief that more money will make everyone happier. Except that it seems that it doesn't. The research on happiness has a remarkable consistency across societies. It seems that where the average income in a society is under ten thousand dollars a year per head then more money does result in more happiness, as recorded by answers to standard questionnaires. Above that level, however, more money does not increase the average levels of recorded happiness. We are talking averages here, across total populations, so we should probably more than double that figure to find the happiness threshold for the average salary earner, but the stark fact remains that above a certain level more money does not make us feel any happier. It makes sense of a sort; once there is enough for the essentials it is often hard to justify the effort needed to earn the extra to buy more of those unnecessary things, particularly if you are independent.

Economists, however, would point out that it is important we continue to believe that more does mean happier, despite the evidence, because unless more people keep on spending more money, our economies will not grow, there will be less to spend on public services and there will be less work and money for the poorer workers, including those in the developing world. It is, you might say, our social duty to spend more than we need to or, perhaps, want to. Odd.

At a personal level, life would be simpler if we followed Aristotle's doctrine of 'enough'. Unless and until we can define what 'enough' is for us in terms of money we will never be truly free – free, that is, to define our real purpose in life. We will, instead, be volunteer slaves to our employer or profession, subordinate to the priorities of others.

Settling for 'enough' does, however, mean that we have to do away with the other uses of money. It will no longer work as a symbol of success, or as a way of defining ourselves, or as an excuse or compensation for not getting on with our real life. We have to become open and honest about what we really value, about how we wish to define ourselves and how we want others to view us. Having tried it, I can vouch for the fact that the honesty it requires of one is refreshing, even if it surprises and disturbs some of our friends who hope that it is not the start of some sort of fashion.

Each September some thirty-five thousand people assemble in the Nevada desert at the week-long Burning Man festival. They come to experience the 'gift economy' in the commerce-free zone that Larry Harvey, the director of the festival, has created there. For a week everything on offer is free. People come to offer their services and goods for free. You can get macaroni and cheese at 4.00 a.m. or be massaged, psychically healed or just sit at a bar and have a beer – and pay nothing. It is, says Larry, a reaction to the overabundance of our modern society and a small attempt to redefine what is really of value.

A full-scale gift economy might not survive more than a week, but one based on 'enough' might be catching as people sense the futility of searching for more when enough would be plenty. The world would then be a more varied and honest place. But then I come up against the economists who worry about the demand curve that creates the supply that translates into jobs and taxes. My compromise is to urge the doctrine of 'enough' on those of us in the 'Third Age', those who have passed beyond the stages of career and family. That is because it gets easier to work out what is enough as one gets older, when there is less need to provide for the uncertainties of the future and while there is still time to do what we feel we are on this earth to do.

At that stage, too, our drop in consumption and earnings won't be significant enough to impoverish the Third World. Our example might be one small strike against the tyranny of money in the modern world. It might give some hope to those who feel that there is no escape from that tyranny. It might even challenge the economists to find a way to break out from the often vicious circles that money creates.

It is pleasing to be released at last from those circles, but I still have problems with 'enough'. Each year Elizabeth and I sit down and work out what we need and what we can anticipate earning. Pessimist that I am I always underestimate the likely income and then overcompensate by taking on more paid work than I need. Twenty years on from leaving Windsor we now live more comfortably than we need to, but I am not complaining. Money is nice as long as it is not the most important thing in life. The truly pressing question I faced as I started to plan my new life, given that I was now going to be a writer, was what I should write about.

A social philosopher, as I now described myself, should, I felt, be concerned with the pragmatic concerns of the emerging society. My immediate ones were also going to be the concerns of more and more people. It seemed clear to me that we were going to have more choices in all areas of our lives. But that would not necessarily make them easier. Confronted by the growing array of cereal packets in the supermarket, most of us do not take the time to compare calorie and sugar counts but go straight to the old familiar ones. In life's new supermarket of abundant choices of how to live and what to do, we either dither hesitantly or, again, go for the old familiar ways and habits when we could be questioning, searching, making the world work for us rather than the other way round. You cannot, however, choose between all those cereal packets unless you have some criterion, some way to sort out the good from the bad. It is no different in the rest of life. Without some criterion, choices just add stress. That, I hoped and believed, was where philosophy might help. That, I said to myself, would be my new role, but I would need to start by applying it to myself as the choices became more urgent.

Chapter Twelve
The Property Business

Cash and a roof over one's head are the essential means of life while, writ larger, property and finance are the fuels of capitalism. My business schools had been dedicated to their study and, as I contemplated life after Windsor, these necessary fuels began to take on a new urgency in my own life.

I think I must have taken the roof for granted in my youth. It was just there, mine not to question how. The Anglo-Irish gentry of my native land were traditionally asset-rich but income-poor, lots of roof with too little cash to stem the leaks. I well remember dining in a fine but decaying Georgian mansion while sitting on an upturned orange box because all the chairs were rotten. My own family did not even have the decaying mansion. The vicarage belonged to the Church. Elizabeth's family was equally asset-free, and proud of it.

'Lend you money for a house? Certainly not. Property? I never touch it. Don't believe in it. Too risky.' That was my father-in-law's response to our request for a small loan to buy a tiny property in Kyrenia, Cyprus, back where we had first got engaged. This was four years before the Turks invaded Northern Cyprus and changed everything. Perhaps, therefore, my father-in-law was proved right in this instance. Mostly, however, he was temperamentally opposed to locking his money away in one large fixed asset. He did not need to. His employer, the army, provided him with housing as he moved around the world serving Her Majesty. My own father, too, had grown up and later lived all his working life in tied houses, the rectories adjacent to the churches where he and his father worshipped.

When it came to my turn I, too, did not think of buying when I forsook the sheltered world of Shell, who had also provided me with housing, even back in Britain. Renting seemed cheaper and, above all, I thought, it kept my options open. I could not sensibly argue with my father-in-law when he poured scorn on our would-be flutter in Cyprus. So when we found a large apartment with a huge garden in South London with a fixed and controlled rental of only thirteen pounds a week I could not believe our luck. We lived there for twelve years at the same price. As an impoverished academic I was delighted with our low outgoings.

Elizabeth was different. Having moved around the world with her parents to a different home every two years, she was longing for a place of her own. She seemed determined to prove her father wrong. And she succeeded. Without my help or, I must admit, my encouragement, she bought a tiny attic apartment in North London on a mortgage, furnished and let it within one week at a rental that more than covered all her outgoings. When she sold it six years later it had increased five times in value. I got the point. I could not object, therefore, when she went off one morning and bought, for almost nothing, a tumbledown uninhabited country cottage for our weekend escapes.

Finally, she had a piece of actual land she could call her own. I was apprehensive. It would cost many thousands of pounds, I could see, to make it habitable and for two years I refused even to visit it. But when, a few years later, our despairing landlord offered to sell us our London apartment at a knockdown price of ten thousand pounds, I knew it was sensible to accept the offer, especially since my father had just died and his legacy just covered that amount. Suddenly, aged forty-five, I was the joint owner of *two* properties. As luck would have it, I then accepted the job in Windsor Castle that came with a tied house included. I was back again in the world of property that I understood, where others bore the costs and the responsibilities.

Imagine, therefore, my amazement and delight, mixed with some considerable degree of guilty confusion about my real beliefs, when, six years after leaving Windsor, a developer offered us £950,000 for our London apartment. Our ten thousand pounds, to which admittedly we had added some refurbishment expenses in the intervening period, had multiplied by a factor of nearly a hundred in ten years. Now I really was a property capitalist. Not my image of myself. Still, it was sexy, this property stuff. While waiting for contracts to be exchanged we made an offer on a fine upstanding house in Notting Hill in London, and, with a quarter of a million pounds still left over, we answered an advertisement in a Sunday paper offering a chance to join a group who were developing a ruined farm in Tuscany. We went out to see the site on our twenty-fifth wedding anniversary, were bowled over by the view and signed on the spot.

We returned to London in time for the fateful first weekend of October in 1987. There was a hurricane on the Friday night in South-East England that flattened woods and flimsy houses and, on Monday, for unrelated reasons, the stock market crashed. Our developer was ruined. The deal on our apartment was off. We withdrew our offer on that fine house in Notting Hill but we were committed to the Italian one. Now I could really begin to sympathise with my father-in-law who, sadly, was no longer alive to say 'I told you so'. By now we had, almost by accident, acquired three homes. This seemed indecent if not actually wrong when so many were homeless.

I have always been conscious of the declaration by Pierre-Joseph Proudhon, the nineteenth-century anarchist, that property is theft. A friend, a Scottish landowner, was once driving an African visitor to his home. Coming round a bend in the road he commented that all the land they could now see belonged to his family.

'What, even that mountain?' asked his visitor.

'Why, yes.'

'But how can you own a mountain?' the African exclaimed in astonishment.

It is a good question, one that has nagged at me down the years. Elizabeth does not share my guilt. Ownership is good, she believes, because if you own something you care for it, you invest in it, you have an incentive to develop it. It is true that during all the years that we rented our London apartment we spent nothing on it, because it wasn't ours. As soon as we owned it we rewired it, replumbed it, repainted it and generally did it up. In Britain, when the Thatcher government began to sell council houses to their tenants, there was an outbreak of new porches, fences and double glazing, all reflecting the pride of new owners and their desire to make the most of their new asset.

We do cherish what we own. But it is usually for our own gain or pleasure, heedless of its effects on others. We have to have planning laws that force us to pay attention to the concerns of our neighbours. In parts of the country we need permission from the local authority to cut down the trees we planted – they are thought to belong now to a wider community than ourselves. The Labour government in Britain felt it necessary to pass a law giving the public the 'right to roam' over agricultural land which, traditionally, belonged exclusively to the farmers who saw it as their own. To enter it without their permission had always hitherto, in Britain, been regarded as trespassing. The Right to Roam Act was an implicit acceptance that land belongs to the nation as well as to the titular owner. The responsibilities of ownership, in other words, reach beyond our own immediate interests, something that it is easy to forget or ignore in our own private nests.

With my social philosopher's cap on, I suggest that it is no different when it is the ownership of a business that is involved. Ownership motivates, it stirs the ambitions and energies of the owners. But it remains intrinsically selfish. If the interests of all the other parties involved are to be respected, fine words and good intentions will not be enough any more than they are in our private dwellings. Laws will be, and are, needed. Corporate social responsibility has all the right language but no teeth. When times get hard, the goodwill gets going.

Capitalism is under attack in many parts of the world, including sectors of our own society. It is seen as exploitative, selfish and uncaring. In one survey eighty-nine per cent of Britons said they felt that managers were only there for their own benefit, while another survey reported that ninety-five per cent of workers did not trust their chief executive. The huge financial rewards paid to senior executives may well be deserved, but the suspicion remains that they are feathering their own nests, scratching each other's backs in their supposedly independent remuneration committees and writing contracts for themselves that provide for huge departure settlements should they fail or be forced to resign.

What has gone wrong? It is tempting to blame the people at the top. Keynes once said, 'Capitalism is the astounding belief that the wickedest of men will do the wickedest of things for the greatest good of everyone.' Keynes was exaggerating. Personal greed perhaps, a lack of sufficient scrutiny of the company's affairs, an insensitivity or an indifference to public opinion, these charges could be levelled against some corporate leaders, but few, thankfully, are guilty of deliberate fraud or wickedness. At worst they were only playing the game according to the new rules. It is these new rules, or, more particularly, the new goalposts that have distorted capitalism.

The stock option, that new favourite child of stock market capitalism, must share a large part of the blame. Whereas in 1980 only about two per cent of executive pay was tied to share options, it is now thought to be over sixty per cent in the US. These executives, not unnaturally, want to realise their options as soon as they can. They are keen to boost the share price in the short term rather than relying on their successors to deliver. The stock option has also acquired a new popularity in Europe as more and more companies go public. To many, however, hugely undervalued stock options are just another way of allowing executives to steal from their companies and shareholders. We raise our eyebrows, sometimes in jealousy but more often in outrage, at the levels of executive remuneration under stock market capitalism.

This is not just a question of dubious individual ethics or of some rogue firms fudging the odd billion. My concern is that the whole business culture may have become distorted. This was the culture that enraptured America for a generation, a culture that argued the market was king, that the shareholder always had priority, that business was the key engine of progress and that, as such, its needs should prevail in any policy decisions. It was a heady doctrine, one that simplified life with its dogma of the bottom line, and in the Thatcher years it infected Britain where it certainly revived the entrepreneurial spirit, but it also contributed to a decline in civic society and to an erosion in the attention and money paid to the non-business sectors of health, education and transport – a neglect whose effects have now returned to haunt the successor governments.

Capitalist fundamentalism may have lost its sheen, but the urgent question now is how best to retain the energy produced by the old model without its flaws. Better and tougher regulation would help. Corporate governance will now surely be taken more seriously by all concerned, with responsibilities more clearly defined, penalties spelt out and watchdogs appointed. But these will be plasters on an open sore, they will not affect the disease that lies at the core of the business culture, which centres around the question 'Who and what is a business for?'. It is a question that every property owner has to face up to if the property is to remain useful.

In a publicly owned business there is, firstly, a clear and important need to meet the expectations of the theoretical owners, the shareholders. But are they true owners? It would be more accurate to call most of them investors, perhaps even punters. They have none of the pride or the responsibilities of ownership and are, if they are truthful, only there for the money. But to turn this need into a purpose is to be guilty of a logical confusion, to mistake a necessary condition for a sufficient one. We need to eat to live, food is a necessary condition of life, but if we lived mainly to eat, making food a sufficient or only purpose of life, we would become gross. The purpose of a business, in other words, is not to make a profit, full stop. It is to make a profit in order to enable it to do something more or better. What that something is becomes the real justification for the existence of the business. Owners know this. Investors needn't care. They are anxious only for their share of that profit.

To many this will sound like quibbling with words. Not so. It is a moral issue. To mistake the means for the ends is to be turned in on oneself, what St Augustine called one of the greatest of sins. Deep down, the suspicions of capitalism are rooted in a feeling that its instruments, the corporations, are immoral in that sense – they have no purpose other than themselves. This may be to do many of them a great injustice, but if so they are let down by their own rhetoric and behaviour. It is a salutary process to ask of any organisation 'If it did not exist, would we invent it?' Only if it was doing something more useful, better or different than anyone else would have to be the answer, with profits as a means to doing just that. John Browne, the chairman of BP, when defending his company's bumper profits in 2004, argued that mutuality was the hallmark of a good business, one in which all involved in it benefited from a profitable enterprise, its customers and employees, the state from the taxes it pays, the environment and, yes, the shareholders. I would go along with that, as long as the benefits were fairly balanced. Mutuality has a long tradition in business but has normally been associated with those organisations that are owned by their members, meaning their customers, like the building societies of Britain who were, for a long time, the principal mortgage providers for middle-income groups.

These organisations existed only to serve their members. Sadly, in my view, many of these societies have in recent years decided to turn their members into investors who behave as rapaciously as any other, concerned only for their own gains. On a much larger scale, organisations like VISA and the Internet are effectively mutuals, they exist only to serve their members. John Browne's use of the term to describe a major corporation is an interesting and useful extension of the term. It might yet become a fashion.

The new legal entity that was formed in Britain in the summer of 2005 may also begin to change how we view a business. This is the Community Interest Company, or CIC. It allows social enterprises to own or use pubic assets – schools, old people's homes, swimming pools and the like – but to guarantee that such properties will always remain in use for the public benefit. Such enterprises can declare a dividend to repay outside investors, and there is now talk of a stock exchange to allow investors to begin to trade their shares. Social enterprises are, in fact, one of Britain's best-kept secrets, making an annual eighteen-billion-pound contribution to the economy and employing seven hundred thousand workers, of whom two hundred thousand are volunteers. They include businesses such as the *Big Issue*, which employs homeless workers to sell its newspaper on the streets, and Greenwich Leisure Limited which has taken a failing service – sport and leisure provision in a London borough – and turned it around, increasing revenue and customers and spreading its scope until it now runs more leisure centres than any other business in the capital. Hackney Community Transport is another social enterprise that consistently tops the customer satisfaction league among London bus companies and wins contracts off its mainstream rivals. Social enterprises put their purpose before their profit while recognising that profit is essential to their survival and growth; it is, as they see it, a tax on the present to pay for their future. More conventional businesses may one day begin to see things the same way.

In the meantime, the best we can do may be to make owners behave as responsible owners. Giving legal force to the responsibilities of the owners may not, however, be enough in the future. Businesses are different from houses or land in one crucial respect: they are largely made up of people, and people, it is generally felt, should not be owned by other people. It may seem to be stretching a point to say that the shareholders actually 'own' the employees, but, increasingly, those employees are the most valuable assets of the business even if they are still classified as costs in the accounts. If the financiers can own the physical assets it seems only logical that they should also be able to own the human ones. It is because this would be an offence against our human rights that the law has, over time, put all manner of restrictions on the use of these ownership powers, but the absolute right to evict these particular villagers from their organisational village remains. Those with the money still own the property.

If I peer into the future it seems likely that the freedom of the owners of companies to do as they please with their property will become increasingly circumscribed by the state, acting in the interest of the wider society, just as it has for the owners of houses and land. The power of the shareholders is also being whittled away from the inside. Share options and huge bonuses may be an expropriation of shareholders' funds and may distort the proper aims of the business, but they are a de facto recognition that an increasing share of the spoils should go to those who worked for them. No longer can the shareholders call all the shots.

More and more far-sighted companies are putting the customers and their employees at the top of the list of their priorities, followed by their obligations to society, as Johnson & Johnson, for example, has always done in its famous credo or statement of values, even if few followed them until now. These companies recognise that their financiers are due a fair return on their investment and assure them that if the other priorities are met that return is likely to be good. The old idea that companies exist to make money for their so-called owners is slowly going out of fashion. A business is, properly, a servant of society, a society of which the owners are a part but not necessarily the main part.

The more I thought about it, the more I wondered whether the language of ownership was the right one to use in the modern world. A company is a community, literally a band of companions. It is not a piece of property, particularly since many companies these days do not themselves own any physical buildings or equipment, may even be almost entirely virtual. Communities are like villages. The physical village can, on rare occasions, be owned by outsiders, but never the villagers. Communities have members, they have obligations, including borrowings or dues owed to investors, and they can themselves own buildings and things, but owners they don't have. Instead, all those connected with them have rights and responsibilities, often recognised by contracts.

It might be, and has been, argued that I am playing with words, that there would be no difference in practice. I disagree. Language matters. If we don't own things like land and companies but only hold them on trust for society, for their members and future generations, then, just perhaps, we might begin to think differently, less selfishly and short term, more considerately of others.

We need capitalism. Even Marx understood that capitalism was the engine of growth in a society, bringing benefits to all. He was worried about who owned that engine. He maintained that the world would not be a just one until the workers owned the means of production. Now they mostly do. It's just that those means of production are in the workers themselves, in their skills, talents, experience and knowledge. Those are now the scarce resource, not money, which is lying around in abundance waiting for useful outlets. Marx was right, albeit unintentionally. We need to give more power to those who make the money, to those who live in the house, and less to those who provide the money, the equivalent of the mortgagers. The first step is to change the language, only then can we begin to adjust the system. Then, just maybe, corporations will begin to be seen as the trustees of our future, which the best of them already are.

Chapter Thirteen
Kitchens and Studies

We have lived in our London apartment on and off for forty years. In that time we have had the kitchen in seven different places. It's cheaper than moving house. Fortunately, the rooms are large and adaptable. We inherited a kitchen in the basement when we moved in, but whereas lugging food up and down stairs might have been fine with servants it was going to be tedious for us, nor did we fancy spending half our time in the gloom of a basement.

So the kitchen moved upstairs to a galley space under the stairs. Then the children came. We wanted to live en famille so converted the guest bedroom into a family kitchen where everything happened. Eight years later when we moved away for four years to Windsor we let the place to a diplomatic couple who needed the family room for a posh dining room, so the kitchen moved again – this time to an efficient streamlined galley. Back again, we converted the garage into a kitchen to give us room for two studies in the main house, now that we were both working from home. Finally, we pulled down the garage and built a modern living space/kitchen down the side of the house, and while we were doing this we had to make a temporary kitchen in one of the bedrooms. Seven kitchens in all.

The details don't matter – even our children can't remember where the kitchen used to be two moves back – but the principle does. We were determined to make our space suit our needs rather than the other way round. We have always been intrigued by the way many of our friends, those who have bought and repaired old houses, still tend to live in what used to be the servants' quarters, keeping the front-of-house rooms for formal occasions, or as a kind of cold storage for their smart furniture. These are houses built for previous generations when the owners lived up front and the servants lived in the kitchen. The live-in servants are gone so our friends now live in their quarters, usually in the badly lit back of the house, facing north with nothing much to see. But that's where the kitchen was, and the kitchen is where most people spend much of their time these days; it's where they perch while they sip or sup.

When I grew up in the vicarage all our meals were eaten in the dining room, even breakfast. The kitchen was for cooking and washing up. It was the maid's territory and I can't remember ever sitting there. The drawing room was used only on Sundays. We huddled round the fire of an evening in my father's study, often interfering with his sermon preparation. The rooms, in short, served their designated purpose at that time – the dining room was for dining, the kitchen for cooking – but I often wonder now how the house may have changed. The current occupant is a bachelor and the maid went long ago. I suspect that the rooms are still the same, but stay mostly cold and unused while he sits like everyone else in the kitchen which did indeed face north and looked out on the coal shed and the backyard.

We, too, live as well as eat in our kitchen, but it is now the most beautiful and sunny room in the house, with space for dining and relaxing as well as cooking and eating. It is, more truthfully, a living room not just a kitchen and the heart of our little family community. We are fortunate to have been able to do this, to have had the rooms and, eventually, the funds. Many, however, adapt their lives to the space rather than the other way round. Often, of course, they have no alternative. Modern houses don't always give one the opportunity to change things. The spaces are all tailor-made to fit the way the developers believe people want to live, which may, nowadays, often combine the living and the cooking, thereby forcing their inhabitants to live as we do, like it or not. The worrying thing is that so many of us are happy to accept the builders' recipes for living instead of demanding more flexibility to fit the space to the way we want to live.

I blame the chimney. In the days before chimneys everyone, masters and servants, children and parents, huddled round the one fire in the big hall under a hole in the roof. Then came the chimney and the possibility of different fires in different rooms, which first split the generations and the social layers. Today there is central heating, which should more properly be termed de-central heating, since it makes it possible for all rooms in the house to be heated simultaneously. Put a microwave and a television in every room and no one need speak to anyone else all day, let alone eat with them.

Many prefer it that way, but the growing popularity of barns and lofts suggests that some at least want to return to the communal spaces of old, or to have more control over the design and use of their personal space. The versatility of our Victorian apartment was as good as that of a barn. The kitchen saga encouraged us to think more about how we should adapt our space to our life as that life changed and developed, our work patterns altered and the children grew up and into homes of their own.

In our apartment what used to be two smart front rooms have now been turned into our private studies, out of bounds to all visitors and even to family. That is because we both work from home and need our separate spaces as well as our communal kitchen. The rooms had better be nice and if that means sacrificing spaces more generally given to smart sitting and formal eating, then so be it. The older traditional description of household space – sitting room, drawing room, dining room – no longer corresponds to the way many of us spend our time, particularly as more and more of us do at least some of our work at home. Squeezing one's workspace into a corner of the dining room, now only rarely used as such, seems illogical and inefficient. Where does one keep the files? Does the computer have to be packed away on the rare occasions that the table is needed for dining?

Organisations have also started to free themselves from the outdated prisons that their buildings have become. The first step was to get the building off the balance sheet by selling it to a property company and leasing it back. This released money for investment in things more directly relevant to the business. I was still at Shell when someone calculated that the company was the largest property owner in Britain, because of all those service stations, in addition to the offices and refineries. Too many businesses had too much of their capital tied up in buildings instead of in the business. Physical assets were still what counted in the accounts, even though the individuals who worked in them were more crucial to their fortunes.

It then began to dawn on people that the office was a major fixed cost that was unused for at least half the time. A chemical plant works twenty-four hours a day. So does a hospital. But the typical office is only open for twelve hours a day at most and often closes at weekends. Even during those twelve hours it is often not fully used. I remember being shown around a newly fashionable office building. I admired the architecture and the interior designs but I couldn't help noticing that more than half the desks and offices were unoccupied. 'Where are all the people?' I asked.

'They are out,' I was told, 'meeting clients, suppliers, looking for ideas, talking to government – working, in fact.' Today they might also be doing some of their work at home.

'You seem to have a lot of wasted space,' I said.

'Not really,' they replied, 'each of these people needs to have their own little place that they can, as it were, call home.' That's nice, I thought to myself, but it's expensive. Indeed, some of those homes away from homes were more luxuriously furnished and equipped than anyone's main home. No wonder some prefer the office to their kitchen at home. But is it really necessary or are they living in an out-of-date world, fitting a modern organisation into old-fashioned spaces?

I thought, then, of teachers I knew, of actors and musicians, of plumbers, taxi drivers and waiters, of gardeners, travelling salesmen and professional sports people – even of my own father, a priest – of all those whose work is done in front of the clients. They don't have private spaces in a building. Teachers may have a mug in the common room and actors a share of a dressing room, but not their own little cave with mugshots of the family. They all have paperwork to do but they do it back home, or in the car. If so much of the modern executive's work is involved with meeting people, perhaps they, too, could dispense with the private space.

Ideas such as these led to the hot-desking policy of some offices, where workers keep any personal belongings in a locker, find a vacant desk when they come in and plug in their computers, pausing just long enough to tell the receptionist where they are parked. It was a rational response to the waste of space in the traditional office, allowing firms to reduce the size of their buildings quite dramatically. But not everyone was happy. The loss of personal space was seen as an affront by many. Some form of variable space is, however, inevitable now that organisations are becoming increasingly dispersed and virtual. In most organisations it is no longer necessary to have all the people in the same place at the same time to get the work done, but we still design many of our offices as if it were. As with houses, we have imprisoned ourselves in the spaces of the last generation.

The office of the future will often be more like a traditional city club. In a club the entry is restricted to members but those members have no spaces they can call their own. Such few private offices as do exist are restricted to those who have to be there all the time, the officers of the club, and those rooms are usually tucked away in the back. All the main rooms have allocated functions – eating, reading, meeting or game playing – but, unless privately booked for a temporary use, they are open to all members and their guests. A club is not a hotel. Only members and their guests are allowed in, but once in, all facilities are available to them. No one expects to have a private room at the club but the premises and the facilities need to be of a certain standard. What the organisation saves on office space it will be able to spend on improving the common services and premises. State-of-the-art telecommunications, decent food and even a gym are essential, but nice furnishings and good art help to make the office a place that people want to come to, even a place they can be proud of belonging to, but no longer will it be a personal home away from home.

There are other options. British Airways has its head office near Heathrow. It operates a modified hot-desking system, one in which groups have an assigned area but no privately allocated spaces within it. They have also tried to give the building the feel of a village. There is a street running down the middle, with a small stream, lined with shops and facilities. There is a café, with tables on the street. None of the buildings is more than three storeys high. The idea is that you have to walk through the street to get to other parts of the organisation, thus encouraging serendipitous meetings and conversations. There is no escalator from the underground car park, forcing drivers to walk through the street to get to their offices. It has an airy, feel-good atmosphere and, although it all looks rather luxurious, British Airways claims that it is energy efficient and cheaper to run than spaces of an equivalent size but more conventional design.

It is a village rather than a club. The design of BA's office was sparked by the discovery that in the old-fashioned head office, long corridors of private rooms behind heavy doors, the executives had filled their diaries with appointments with other executives who lived behind their own heavy doors. It was hoped that opening up the space would also open up the organisation. As always, the reaction of the old guard was negative. No one likes to lose their private space, but in time those who have known nothing else will take clubs or villages in their stride.

Few need privacy to do their job and where it is necessary there are rooms set aside for the purpose. Go to meet your lawyer and you will usually be shown into a private meeting room, not to the lawyer's desk.

It is easy to forget that the original partners' desks were two-sided, so that two partners could sit facing each other, typically in a room shared by six to eight partners in order to keep everything as open as possible, to make communication as easy and immediate as possible. The modern equivalent is the trading floor of a big bank, where the need to share information with other traders in order to keep abreast of a fast-moving situation means that they all share a common space.

We are seeing a return to the idea of the commons – a common space shared by members – to our organisations, even while it is eroding in much of our private life. One has to wonder how it came about that we began to enclose our organisational commons. Probably for the same reason that the enclosures happened on the old commons, because territory gave power and status with the result that those who could get it, got it. The old stories of status being marked out by the size of office, the fitted or non-fitted carpet, the tea tray not the tea urn, the officers' mess not the canteen – these fabled tales of the importance of space and its symbols were still a reality in my early days in Shell. I can recall the frustration I felt when a meeting broke up at lunchtime, when half of those present would go to their senior mess for lunch to continue the debate upstairs while the rest of us queued up in the basement canteen, knowing that we were now effectively excluded from the discussion.

Those days have long gone, but territory still matters, in homes as well as in offices. I sympathise with those who rue the loss of private space. I and my wife both need ours. We could not work together unless we had our own private spaces as well as a common territory – the kitchen, where we meet for agenda setting and problem solving. We each do creative work for which some isolation seems to be essential. Creative problem solving, on the other hand, seems to work better when done together or in a group. The answer, therefore, has to be spaces for cases, rather than one solution for all. Most offices will then end up with a mix of both private and communal. What proves to be interesting is how the senior people define their own jobs – are they mainly creative or are they problem solving? If the latter they will sit in full view in the middle of the office. If the former they will shut themselves away in their own cell.

Some organisations solve the problem by allocating spaces for creative thinking, reading or writing, rooms without telephones or email connections, comfortably furnished but isolated, soundproofed and available to all on request. Other organisations expect you to do your solo work at home, using the office for joint problem solving, communication and meetings. It is both possible and sensible to use different spaces for different activities. All offices need some mixture of our studies and kitchen. The challenge, as always, is one of balance.

In our own life we have carried the idea of spaces for cases one step farther. We find that London has too much going on for the isolation that our creative work seems to need. For that we retreat to the country cottage we bought thirty-five years ago as a holiday home. There, in the middle of East Anglian fields, we are undisturbed. London then becomes the place for activity, for meetings and the personal contacts that all work needs. Separating your spaces by a hundred miles is inconvenient and not to be recommended unless you are as undisciplined as we are. Any closer and the temptation to respond to any urgent problem, opportunity or invitation would be too great. All the best parties and shows seem to be programmed to happen in our country spells; too close to town and we would succumb. Others are more self-disciplined. Some seem to be able to squeeze their creative work into the cracks in their daily chores, scribbling while the children squabble or on the train to work. We find that we need to shut ourselves away in our country space to get the work done, using space as an organising discipline.

The next step for us, if we really want to practise what we preach, must be to cut down our London space to just a bedroom and a living area, for sleeping, cooking and communing. The old separate study spaces in London are now, if we are honest, superfluous. We are, therefore, in the process of selling our large apartment to our daughter and her partner, accepting, in part exchange, her garden apartment in the same building. She and her husband need our studies for their consulting rooms and we no longer use them much.

It is, I am uncomfortably aware, one more sign of the passing years, this inter-generational transfer. We are lucky that we only have to move next door. Shall I, I ask myself, look on with regretful envy as my daughter and her husband enjoy our old spaces? Or will I rejoice in the greater simplicity of our lives? I must remind myself that it is a foolish futility to envy the young. Better by far to enjoy watching their lives grow, particularly if it is in our old spaces, even if they don't seem to want any of the family treasures that we have so carefully hoarded for them down the years.

One enormous plasma screen is now screwed to the wall above the fireplace, replacing the painting that once hung there when it was still our home. It is a stark reminder that their tastes and priorities are, naturally, different from ours. So will be the uses that they will make of our old spaces.

Space and Time we now know are interconnected in space. So it is in life. My wife and I have tried to shape the use of our time as well as our spaces to fit the life we want to live. There is no need for us or anyone to live by the formula that suited the agricultural age. As more and more organisations move towards the 24/7 life, they have had to require their workforce to adapt to chunking their lives in untraditional ways. This is nothing new for hospitals, airlines, police forces or taxi drivers but now more and more of the workforce is on some sort of shift system. For the bulk of the population Sunday is as busy as any other day, even if most of us use it for shopping.

Some years back we calculated that if you add together the fifty-two weekends, the twenty days of paid annual leave that most people get and the eight public holidays, we are all entitled to 132 free days each year, over a third of all the days in the year, all on full pay. That's a lot. It is a puzzle why some people want to add to it with 'duvet days' and false sick days. They must find their work truly distasteful or stressful. One of the delights of being an independent worker is that you slice those 132 free days any way you like. You could, if it suited, take a three-month break every year and still have Sundays off in the remaining weeks. Two annual holidays are now commonplace and some organisations allow sabbatical chunks. Alternatively, you can, of course, regard 132 days as excessive and allocate half or most of them to work, sensible if money worries you.

In our case we decided to allocate one hundred and fifty days to our purely creative work, writing and photography, along with the reading and research that goes with both. We then allowed one hundred days to administration and business, mostly foreign lecture tours, with a sort of tithing allowance of thirty days for voluntary work of one sort or another. That still leaves eighty-five days free for one day off a week and the odd break. We keep a check on the totals but which days of the week are used for which is irrelevant. In fact we usually keep Fridays free for leisure interests of one sort or another, and work most Sundays when the phone doesn't ring. It requires self-discipline to keep to the allocations. It is tempting, for instance, to add to the business days because that means money, but we know that without the investment in the writing and photography there would soon be no business. These are the R & D of our life and must be protected.

In an ideal world, the allocation of the 132 days off and the 233 days of work should be the joint choice of employer and individual. An annual hours contract of, say, 1,600 hours, makes that choice possible although in practice it is always the organisation's preference that prevails. That need not be so. The thirty-five-hour week introduced by the socialist government in France forced organisations to discuss the split with their employees and to be more creative in their use of time. The law did not, as intended, increase the number of jobs, and was unpopular, understandably, with small employers, but it markedly improved the quality of life of many individuals, allowing them more choice in balancing their lives, to be at home on Wednesdays, for instance, when children are not at school all day, or, as some did, to take on another part-time job to increase their income. Happier individuals do not always make more productive workers but French productivity per hour per worker was the highest in Europe during this period.

In a looser more flexible world of work, both space and time are up for grabs. In Britain eight million people, thirty per cent of the workforce, now work from home for part of the time. More would like to do so. They have the chance, a chance denied to most of their parents or grandparents, to shape their times and places of work to fit their needs instead of the other way round. We should not be imprisoned by the patterns of the past but design our use of both to suit ourselves, whether we are organisations or individuals. It brings more of life under our own control.

Chapter Fourteen
Kennels for Kids

'You British are strange,' my Dutch friend said, 'you keep your dogs at home but send your children to kennels.' Strange, too, that these kennels, the public boarding schools that are actually private, should be seen by many as the best form of education and worth paying the huge and growing fees that they charge for sheltering our offspring from the ugly world outside and, perhaps more crucially, from their parents.

Both our children, the girl and the boy, spent a part of their teenage years in these educational kennels. Why did we do it? Because that was the way it had been for us and because we believed, along with most of our friends, that they were the best schools around. That was despite my feelings that it was wrong in principle to be able to buy privilege for one's children. Still, as a friend reassured me, I would not be the first to sacrifice my principles for my children. Looking back, I am surprised that I did not reflect more on my own experience before imposing something similar on our children.

I was sent away at age nine and thereafter, for the next ten years, I saw my home and my parents only in the school holidays. The schools were too far away, one was in another country, to allow me to return during term-time. I was always going to be a part-time member of my family, an outsider, albeit a much loved one. The result was that I never knew my parents as well as I would have liked. They weren't there, couldn't be there, when I needed them, nor was I there to share in their lives and to learn from their example.

Besides, I hated my schooling. I was bullied and beaten. I hated the lack of privacy. I was never in a room of my own, by day or night. Always there were others sharing the limited space, boys only, and mostly not of my choice. Even the lavatories had the doors taken off them, in case we got up to no good. I could do the work well enough. With a good short-term memory I could hold things in my head long enough to write them down in an examination. But I was hopeless at sport. My best achievement was to be the scorer for the First XI, the school cricket team. To be good in class and bad on the games field was the wrong way round in those schools. I wasn't one of the gang. Outsider at school and at home, I felt very much alone. When I told my mother all this many years later she was astonished.

'But you never said anything.'

'Of course not. I just assumed that this was how it was meant to be.'

School, my parents had told me, was a preparation for life. But if this was life, I didn't think I was going to enjoy it much.

Nor, in retrospect, did it do much to prepare me for that life. Like many, I claim that I learnt nothing that I now remember at my schools. That isn't strictly correct. It is true that nothing much that I learnt for those examinations has stayed with me. I had to relearn anything that was valuable all over again in later life. But schools, particularly those types of boarding schools, have two curricula: there is the formal, explicit curriculum that lays down what is to be taught in the classroom, but there is also another implicit curriculum, one seldom spelt out or written down. A school is where the child is first exposed to a formal organisation or meets any adults other than relatives for the first time. It is where one learns about power and who holds it, about the pitfalls as well as the pleasures of relationships, whom to trust and whom to avoid. There are lessons here about how to succeed and what counts as success. Amongst other things, I learnt, I thought, that adults knew best, that they, the teachers, the experts, understood the world and that my job was to learn what they knew and remember it.

The problem was that this implicit curriculum was often misleading. To collaborate was called cheating. So was looking things up in a book, or, today, on the Internet, instead of trying to keep it all in your head. In later years I had to unlearn those lessons very speedily if I was to survive in business, where collaboration and the verification of facts were both essential. Age, I was to discover later, was not necessarily correlated with wisdom. Elders, including teachers, did not always know the answers. But they still had the power, so it paid to do what they said even though I knew it was wrong. It took me several years after leaving to start to trust my own judgment, and I still have a tendency to accept, without much questioning, what officials tell me. Governments know best, I used to think. Not always, I now realise.

So why, knowing all this and having experienced all that, did I concur with the decision to send our children to one of these places? Because, although I questioned it, I was still brainwashed enough to go along with the accepted wisdom of my generation, in case they might be right. I didn't want our children to lose out.

Besides, I said to myself, the best of those places are better than in my time. They have done a lot to make the implicit curriculum both explicit and more relevant.

Schools of all types now claim to develop the whole individual. Citizenship is now a course, not just a wished-for outcome. I remember the huge 'Aha!' effect on me when I first read Professor Howard Gardner's theory of multiple intelligences, which demonstrated that one could be intelligent in many different ways. 'Of course,' I said, as did many teachers and schools who went on to adapt their programmes to cater for a wider range of abilities. I still don't think that most of them go far enough. Part of the reason is that there are no measures to assess whether, in the long term, schools are achieving what they say they are trying to do – to produce well-rounded, competent citizens, able to exercise all their talents. As it is, the formal measures only calibrate academic achievement and, since, as the old adage goes, what gets counted is what counts, the old traditional intelligences still dominate. Almost in spite of the wishes of the teachers, schools are increasingly focused on getting their students good grades in their examinations. As so often, targets and league tables distort the real aims of the activity.

Twenty years ago I was chairman of a campaign called Education for Capability at the Royal Society of Arts. Founded by a small group of educationalists and businessmen, it was an expression of our concern that there was a serious imbalance in British education at that time. The idea of the educated person, both then and now, was that of the scholarly individual, taught to understand but not to act. 'A well-balanced education,' our published manifesto said, 'should of course embrace analysis and the acquisition of knowledge. But it must also include the exercise of creative skills, the competence to undertake and complete tasks and the ability to cope with everyday life, and to do all these things in co-operation with others. Educators should spend more time preparing people in this way for a life outside the education system.' One hundred business, political and education leaders signed our manifesto but much of the education system was unimpressed. 'They have to pick up those other skills in the street,' one teacher told me.

Spreading the word of what we called 'capability', I was invited to address the staff of one of the better known public schools. When I had concluded my spiel, the headmaster thanked me, commenting that it was clear that I would not endorse much of what went in their classrooms but that I might approve of what happened when classes finished and they went off to play team sports, to drama classes or the school orchestra, to do community work or tackle a project on the Duke of Edinburgh's Award Scheme.

Indeed, I replied, but you are unusual in that you have to keep the boys and girls busy because you are in charge of them for twenty-four hours a day. You are obviously filling those extra hours with good capability-type activities. Pity those, therefore, that leave the premises when classes finish and have to pick up the other skills elsewhere if at all; the students, in other words, in the state sector, which accounts for over ninety per cent of education in Britain. I argued then that in all schools the day should be divided in half, with classes ending at midday and the afternoon given over to extra-curricular activities, not necessarily led by the same teachers but bringing in other types of professional or experienced help from the surrounding community. It is beginning to happen, belatedly, in Britain where, in 2005, the Education Secretary, Ruth Kelly, announced a policy to keep all schools open until 6.00 p.m. in order to allow more such activities to happen. Whether there will be enough money to turn her wishes into reality has yet to be seen.

I was to discover, however, that there were deeper underlying problems in the implicit curriculum. In the early eighties I was invited by the then Schools Council in Britain to take a look at schools as organisations. Were their systems, management approaches and structures appropriate? How did they strike me as organisations, given my theoretical knowledge of these beasts – I had recently published *Understanding Organisations* – and my practical experience of working in and with a variety of other types of organisation, albeit mainly business ones?

I set off to visit a few of them one wet and cold November, greatly helped by the then director of education in Coventry, Robert Aitken, who got me into a range of different schools in his area. There is nothing more pleasurable, I then discovered, on a cold wet morning than dropping in on a small primary school. Everyone was so clearly having fun, reminding me that you learn little if you aren't enjoying it. The young students sat in groups working on projects together. It looked not unlike the groups you might find in a design studio or an architects' office.

It seemed a different world when I moved down the road to the large comprehensive secondary school. I still remember walking into the staff room and, trying to make conversation while we drank our coffee, asking how many people worked there. 'About seventy, I think,' they replied. I was surprised. This was a large school after all. When I told the story to Robert Aitken he said, 'Oh dear, they left out the cleaners.' 'No,' I said, 'they left out the children.'

To me it was an eye-opener. Looking at that school as an organisation, as I had been asked to do, it was clear that the children were the products in some sort of factory. They were treated, organisationally, as raw material to be processed, passing through various workstations called classes, tested, examined and graded before being despatched, a process that normally lasted from five to seven years. The better the raw material was to start with, the more likely it was that a good grade would result at the end.

It was a stereotype of a school, I realise. It was and is a cruel way of picturing a school, where many dedicated teachers are doing all they can for every young student. My contention was that the way schools are set up makes their job more difficult than it should be. If the students were treated, organisationally, as workers, as they seemed to be in the primary schools I had visited, the atmosphere would be very different.

Workers in well-organised factories and offices have particular tasks to do. They work on projects for much of the time, in conjunction with other workers. Their tasks normally have a beginning and an end. They can see for themselves when they succeed or fail. They are not afraid to ask for help. They know themselves what they can do best and what others can do better. If they are sensible they collaborate. A good organisation makes sure that they have learnt all the skills and techniques that they need to do the job. The teachers are project supervisors as well as instructors with a major role in designing projects that their students will see as interesting and relevant. On one of my tours to inspect projects nominated for an award, I spoke to a young man who was studying the manufacture of quality glassware in an art college. 'What sort of diploma do you get at the end of the course?' I asked.

'I'm not sure,' he said, 'but this is the only diploma I need,' and he pointed to the beautiful piece of glassware he had just finished making. The end product was reward enough.

Such a way of thinking would turn the idea of a school upside down. It would not be easy to run such a place, although some are now trying. In picturing an extreme, however, I was arguing that the way schools are designed goes against the grain of human nature. I firmly believe that we can learn anything, provided that we want to enough. The problem is that most of what we are asked to learn in schools does not excite or interest us. We are asked to take it on trust that it will be useful to us in some distant future, and when you are fifteen, thirty is an age away, out of sight and of mind. As I had discovered for myself, warehoused or stockpiled learning goes off rapidly. All lessons should have a 'use by' label attached if they are going to stick.

Seven-year-olds can text on their mobiles better than I can, use an iPod, programme a video – clearly, they can learn to read and count if they can see that they need to. The Harry Potter books would not have sold so many copies if the young didn't want to read them. If there are exceptions it is because their parents and their schools have not found what turns them on. We have to work with the grain of our children's interests not ours, to start where they are, not where we are. As it is, children are learning anyway, although it may not be what we want them to learn. As I used to remark in my Education for Capability speeches, 'There is a lot of learning going on in society, the trouble is that most of it is not in schools.' It has always been thus. We learn most when we are working on things that interest us, and for most people those things aren't in schools.

One of the people portrayed in our 'New Alchemists' book more than proved the point. She is Sabrina Guinness, the founder of Youth Culture TV back in 1994. YCTV took young people aged between eleven and nineteen and trained them in every aspect of television work, including presenting the programmes, culminating in the production of a half-hour broadcast each week. This was education for reality, designed principally for young people disillusioned with traditional schooling. Whether they ended up with a job in the media or not, said Sabrina, they left believing in themselves, with enhanced self-discipline and a set of practical and personal skills that will always stand them in good stead. It was serious stuff. Anyone applying had first to go through a four-day induction course followed by a series of technical workshops. Only then did they get to work on the actual broadcast programmes. The youngsters who were disenchanted with school queued up to get on Sabrina's courses – because it was something they wanted to learn.

Our studies of the 'New Alchemists' taught us something else, that schools matter but families matter more. Research consistently shows that the family background has more effect on classroom grades than any type or level of school. The research results show that children who come from more affluent backgrounds tend to do better in their studies. Other research has shown that where families are involved the performance of the student improves. But I suspect it goes deeper than that. The family, whatever form it takes, is our first and, for a longish time, our only model of how the world works, how people relate to each other, of what is right and what is not acceptable.

The attitudes and expectations of the parents had an important bearing on the lives of the alchemists. Early responsibility as a child, the chance to test one's curiosity by experiment, to learn that mistakes are not fatal and that change can be exciting, these were the initial seeds of alchemy – stifle them and you risk stunting the creative impulses of the young child. Only three in our sample of twenty-nine were firstborn. There weren't more of these eldest children, perhaps, because parental expectations of traditional achievement weighed too heavily upon the firstborn. They may have been successful but many did not have the experimental cast of mind that makes one an entrepreneur or a creative. To experiment with life you need a bit of freedom.

As it is, there are more and more signs today that children are being overprotected, particularly in the big cities. Ferried everywhere in cars or buses, guarded from strangers, prevented even from playing with friends in case they are hurt and sue their hosts, there is often nothing left for experimental youngsters except computer games in the security of their own homes. A 1999 BBC study of 1,300 young people found that they were fed up with being oversupervised and corralled by parents and teachers. In a speech that I once made as chair of a big education conference, I suggested that we should be more relaxed about naughty children in our schools, as long as they did not harm anyone. It might, I said, be the only way they could experiment. The remark earned me a stern rebuke from one of the teachers' unions who warned me to keep my distance from their classrooms.

Families matter more than schools, however. Schools occupy only fifteen per cent of our waking time over the year. Families take up most of the rest. They may think they have no influence over their unruly teenagers but, for good or ill, their example is a powerful teacher. It can be no coincidence that both our children have chosen to work as independents. As our daughter put it, 'I like working with people but not for them.' They grew up seeing how we, their parents, lived and worked and now they both do likewise, working from home with their partners. It cannot be accidental that it is the sons and daughters of divorced parents who are more likely than others to get divorced themselves. What would be unthinkable in my own family is seen as normal in others. If you grow up in a musical household the chances are that you will love music, particularly since your genetic inheritance will probably incline you that way. The best predictor of anyone's occupation used to be what their father or mother did. Only now, with so many occupations unknown to the parents, has the link been weakened, but not extinguished. My ancestors were preachers. I stand on platforms, speaking to conferences. Our son claims that he is the only honest member of the family because he actually calls himself an actor. We have always been performers, actors of a sort, he points out, whether we called ourselves bishops, archdeacons or professors. He may be right. It is in our blood, and in our family habit.

Families influence occupations and interests, but also, and importantly, values. It is alarming, and occasionally pleasing, to see your attitudes reflected in your children. My wife and I always rated our interest in a job above the money, as long as we had just enough to survive, but were both pleased and a little worried when we saw our children take the same attitude. Would they really have enough, when enough was nowadays set rather higher than in our own youth? I once suggested to our actor son that acting was better as a leisure activity than as a career, that maybe he should think of becoming a barrister, which still, I argued, contained elements of the stage. He looked at me in amazement. 'I can't believe you said that, you who always said you should go where your heart is, not the money.'

Who we are always speaks louder than what we say. The way we walk is more memorable than the way we talk. When I now reflect on the influence of the family for good or, sometimes, for ill, I wonder why we were so ready to delegate the youth of our children to strangers. A perceived inadequacy was one reason. I remember thinking that if our son went to a local day school I would be largely responsible for his after-school life. I feared that I would have neither the energy, the time nor the spread of interests to keep him engaged. I worried that he would find companions and mentors not of my choosing, that he would be, in short, out of my control. Instead we sent him away to one of those kennels and, in retrospect, lost him for a while. Having delegated so much of his care and development to others, he was now even more beyond my influence. Looking back I am ashamed of my cowardice.

What sort of society are we growing, I wonder, when so many parents find it easier to hand over the development of their young to people they don't really know, in crèches, playgroups, schools? Schools of one sort or another are necessary. With few exceptions families cannot, and perhaps should not, be the only ones responsible for what the French call the 'formation' of their young. Schools do teach some useful and necessary things. Even if we forget most of them, something remains but not, sadly, always the bits we expected. That implicit curriculum can be more powerful than the official one. Families teach more than they know but, sadly, not all families should be teachers. There are bad families, non-existent families, lazy families and poor families. Schools can be a safety net for the children from such homes.

Most crucially, we need schools to teach us how to think, now that all rules are up for grabs with the decline of the traditional sources of authority, the religions and the elders of the community. It is easy to forget how engrained have been the traditions of religion in our society even among those who professed no faith. The Christian story, in particular, provided an accepted backcloth to Western lives, bearing with it so many of the rules that govern our behaviour. 'Do unto others as you would have them do unto you' and 'Love your neighbour as yourself' are just two of them. We may not act on these precepts but we know them. If the mythology is forgotten, the messages it carries go, too.

If religions are losing their grip in the Western mind and relativism is on the rise, people have to be taught how to make up their own minds. You can do that in any subject if you are presented with problems rather than facts. But one subject concentrates solely on thinking. People, both young and old, need, in short, to study philosophy. Families exude their own philosophy by their example but they will find it difficult to teach their own to think independently, usually because they don't know how to do so themselves. It is a difficult challenge, but rather than preaching a particular philosophy under the label of 'citizenship' I would like to see the schools develop courses in philosophy to which all generations were welcome.

The courses I am envisaging would not be shortened versions of the works of the great philosophers but would be more akin to the essays I had to write at university, posing questions that need answering. Nor need there be essays. Group discussions are more suitable. Take, as one possible discussion, the question of 'What is Justice?'. Justice can mean giving people what they deserve by way of reward or punishment, pay for performance, perhaps, or, on the other hand, fines for breaking the law. But justice can also mean giving people what they need. A graduated tax, for instance, leaves the poor with more of their earnings. Most people would see this as just, but if it goes too far the rich feel that they are being treated unjustly. Where is the balance? Some philosophers, John Rawls in particular, argue that the basic principle should be equality. Only if the many benefit should some be rewarded unequally. It may be just, they might argue, for doctors to be paid more because the population needs more doctors for the benefit of all.

As with all philosophical questions there are no right answers, only an investigation of the issues and the challenge to be clear where you stand yourself. If we don't know where we stand on the big issues of morality and ethics, we lay ourselves open to those who want to impose their definitions on us, or to a laissez-faire attitude of anything goes. Both are dangerous.

I am not optimistic that many schools will pick up the philosophical agenda, although some primary schools have made a start. The problem lies in the way that we have chosen to measure learning. Philosophy is not a set of right or wrong answers that can be ticked and scored. It is the process, not the outcome, that matters – how the argument is developed and the conclusion justified. The only answers that matter in philosophy are the ones you work out for yourself. That makes it hard to grade, hard to set standards, hard to find enough teachers prepared to give it the time it deserves. Sometimes, however, we have to do things just because they are right or necessary. Philosophy is a core course in French schools. Perhaps that is why the pragmatic British will have none of it. That being so, the family will always remain the main influence on our lives, showing us how to think as well as how to live, something I increasingly appreciate as I watch our two children in their adult lives.

Chapter Fifteen

Family Matters

'Beware,' I told our son as he contemplated marriage, 'it won't be just the love of your life that you will be marrying, but a whole new family. You had better know what you are getting into; families matter, as you will discover.'

I was speaking from personal experience. I had met Elizabeth one rain-sodden night at a party in Kuala Lumpur. It never occurred to me then, or for some time later, to enquire where she came from or what her family consisted of. She was more than enough in herself – until things started to get serious. She invited me down to stay with her parents in Singapore, where her father was serving with the British Army. It was soon all too obvious that this family was rather different from the one I had left behind in the Irish vicarage. 'Are you sleeping with my daughter?' the colonel inquired as he offered me a drink in the sitting room soon after I arrived. We were alone. I sensed it was a test of a sort. Discretion, I felt, would definitely be the better part of truth on this occasion, so, blushing, I smiled and said, 'Thank you, whiskey and a touch of water would be fine.' He looked me up and down. 'Hmmph,' he said and handed me the whiskey.

He was a glamorous man, Elizabeth's father, as was her mother. They were party animals with a host of friends and wonderful company. I was enthralled by their carefree attitude to life, their slanderous jokes, irreverent gossip and their generosity to all and sundry. They lived life very differently to my parents. I loved it and they were kindness itself to me. That was until I proposed to their daughter. As one of her swains and admirers I passed muster. Joining their family was something else again. They were holidaying in Turkey when we, back in London now, wrote to say we were engaged and hoped for their pleased approval. A letter arrived eventually, addressed to Elizabeth. What's the hurry, it said, you are young and there are other fish to fry. Looking back now, they were right in a way. I didn't fit. They wanted something better for their only daughter, maybe an ex-officer with a country estate to inherit, not the impecunious son of an Irish pastor, who had turned down the chance to serve in the army. But just in case, the colonel got a fishing companion of his, a senior manager in Shell, to look up my file and check out my prospects. Quite outrageous, I felt, when he told me what he had done, even though the result seemed to have reassured him, although he commented, having also studied Shell's pension plan, that I seemed to be worth more dead than alive.

We married six months later, but the early omens weren't good. Anxious to do the right thing I had ordered a large expensive limousine to drive my future mother-in-law to the church in the City where we were to be married – St Mary Aldermary, opposite Mansion House Tube station and conveniently near to the Tallow Chandlers' Hall where the reception was to be held. Unfortunately, the chauffeur took her to St Mary Aldermanbury. An understandable mistake perhaps, but as luck would have it that church was in the process of being dismantled brick by brick to be reassembled in America. My mother-in-law, who disapproved of the wedding anyway, looked out to see a church with no roof and half of its walls gone. She was not amused.

Fifteen years later, sadly and too soon, my father-in-law died, before he had time to drink the thirty-three cases of excellent claret he had stored away with his wine merchant for his retirement. In his will, I was thrilled to discover, he had left most of them to me. Over the years I have turned over this treasure trove, selling some and investing in more and newer wines for the future. Each time we drink it, I privately raise my glass in gratitude, for the wine but, even more, for its message, as I read it, that I had finally earned my right to belong to his family, a family that is now as treasured by me as my own Irish one. Even my mother-in-law came around eventually.

Entering a new family is not unlike going to live in another country. You have to learn their ways and customs and earn the right to residence whilst still retaining your own identity. Like countries, families have their histories, which shape their cultures. When I got engaged my future mother-in-law sent my parents a copy of the family history written by an ancestor of her husband. My mother, not to be outdone, responded with an account of her family. My guess is that they were exchanging more than information. Nor are weddings always the joyous occasions they seem. There can be colourful clashes of cultures as each side sums up the other, leaving the newly married couple to bridge the gap. That gap never quite closes. As an in-law I know that, despite my best efforts, I will always have only the equivalent of a green card in my new family and will be a resident by adoption rather than by right of birth. That's only as it should be. Families guard their boundaries carefully. If they don't they soon cease to be the safe refuge in time of trouble that the best of them are.

During those early months of courting my future wife, I realised that you don't fully know someone until and unless you know their family. So much of who we are is tied into our genetic inheritance. So much of the way we think and behave is determined by what we picked up in our early years. Odd then, that we often hide our families away from our friends. Ashamed? Scared of what they might reveal about us? I hesitated to bring back my smart university friends to my more modest home in Ireland. What would they think of our unsophisticated ways, of those family prayers around the breakfast table each morning, for instance, or tea instead of wine or beer with meals? To my relief and surprise those friends who did come loved it all, adored my parents and even joined in those breakfast prayer meetings. It was partly, I suspect, because they understood me better, or maybe because I could finally relax once they knew the truth about where I came from. Most people, I now observe, seem more real to me once I meet their close family. Only then do I see them in the round, without the protective screen of their public persona, the mask that we all wear until we know someone well enough to take it off. The best compliment that anyone can pay me today is to introduce me to their parents or their siblings.

It takes time, however, to grow into a family, to accept that they are an inescapable fact of your life and should be appreciated as such. As long as my mother-in-law was alive her extended family would gather in the week before Christmas to exchange gifts and greetings. It could be a fraught occasion, one to which few of us looked forward but which we miss now that the matriarch has gone and the tradition has lapsed. The mere fact that we have the same roots will never guarantee that we have the same values or interests. Families aren't always easy. And yet, and yet. When you need them, like them or not, they are the people most likely to be there for you. I remember the huge sense of loss when the second of my parents died. I was now an orphan. I remember, too, the shattered face of an old friend, my age, when his only sibling died and he was left without any of his own old family. Like them or loathe them, we need our families.

That seems to be true even if they are not the conventional family of 2.2 kids from the same parents. The variety of family shapes and sizes is now mind-boggling. Our own two children used to complain that whereas most of their friends were debating which parent to go to for Christmas, they had no choice. I once made the mistake of talking about my, not our, daughter. 'Does your wife have a daughter too?' was the response, assuming that I was in one of those families where each partner contributes children from a previous relationship. Co-habitation, divorce and serial monogamy are creating more reconstructed family units. In 2001 ten per cent of all families in the UK were stepfamilies and thirty per cent were not headed by two adults. The new families can even be easier than the traditional ones, because less is expected of its members.

Perhaps we are just living longer. In Victorian times the typical marriage lasted just fifteen years because one partner, often the wife, died early. Now they don't die, they leave, but fifteen years remains the average length of a marriage, some longer, some shorter. 'Till death us do part' may have been a realistic promise in earlier days. Now many couples prefer to vow to stay together 'as long as our love lasts'. That nicely begs the question: what is love? Giving more unwanted advice to my son I urged him not to settle for passion or physical attraction as the basis for a long-term relationship but to look for someone who would one day end up as his best friend, in a friendship that could deepen as life went on. One day, I told my unbelieving offspring, it won't be great sex that he will want in bed but hugs and cuddles. I was not just speaking from personal experience. Long before, I had set out to investigate, with the help of a research assistant, how some of my married executive students at the business school were coping with the stress of combining successful careers and stable marriages. The research led me to conclude that good marriages subtly change the underlying contracts that partners have with each other as their lives develop.

These days I sometimes quip that I am now on my second marriage – but to the same woman. When the children grew up and began to lead their own lives, when all four of our parents had died, along with the dog, my wife and I were suddenly free once again to develop our own lives. The family bonds that had done so much to hold us together and had provided a common strand to our daily life had weakened. It can be a challenging time of transition. We had a history together. Did we have a future together? I was building an independent life as lecturer, broadcaster and writer. Elizabeth had just finished a degree in Photography and would now have the time to develop a full professional life. We could both be comfortably busy, but leading largely separate lives. Some couples, we knew, whose working lives had diverged, saw this as the time to find new partners who would build a new life with them, often centred around common interests in their work. We had too much invested in each other to want to risk this happening to us.

So we decided to find a way to combine our work and so preserve our friendship, our marriage and our family, all things precious to us. She manages my work, acts as my agent and organises our engagements, travelling everywhere with me. I add my words to her photographs and her books and help out as best I can on her photo shoots. As one result we are always together, joined at the hip. A consultant once expressed his sympathy for what he called the loneliness of the travelling lecturer's spouse and enquired of Elizabeth what was the longest spell that I was apart from her. 'Forty minutes,' she replied, 'when he's at the supermarket.' Such perpetual proximity might not be to everyone's taste but we find it pleasing to think that there is no one whom either of us meets who is not known to the other, that all our experiences are shared and no nights are spent alone. There can be no secrets in such an arrangement. We have found in it a new sort of intimacy, one based on mutual trust more than a shared passion. It was truly a new marriage, but made with the same partners. It is more comfortable that way, and cheaper.

A marriage, or its modern-day equivalent of long-term cohabitation, is one essential building block of a family. But it can be, indeed should be, according to the English prayer book, only the prelude to the next and more difficult stage, that of parenting. I was not one of those who longed for children. That, I felt, might well be one commitment too far. I remember sitting by my wife as she gave birth to our first child and thinking, as I saw the nurse lift up my new daughter, 'That's going to keep me working for the next twenty years.' Buying a house is bad enough, but you can always trade it in if you don't like it. A daughter was something else again. There would be no escape from this commitment, no way to trade it in or sell it on.

Half an hour later I forgot all that. With a sudden gulp of joy I knew what people meant by unconditional love. There would be difficult times ahead, I realised that, and new challenges for me, but I would never, I knew then, cease to love that funny bald-headed bundle whatever she did or did not do. To love and seek for no return is altruism at its best, but this time it came unbidden.

That was just as well, because parenting proved to be more difficult than I imagined. To my dismay it did not come naturally. Bringing up children is difficult and I don't suppose we did it particularly well. But the most difficult dilemmas start when they pass out of your control. There was that ominous day when I laid down the law about something now forgotten, only for my six-year-old to rebuke me, 'But Miss Gotto says . . .' and I knew that I was outgunned. Miss Gotto was her teacher and the ruling authority in her life. I was just the man who came to lunch on Sundays. Our son saw me differently. His class at primary school were once asked to write a short essay on 'What My Daddy Does'.

'What did you say?' I asked, curious how he would describe my job at the business school.

'I said you were a painter.'

Hmm. Interesting. Maybe he had detected a hidden artistic streak in me. 'What did you say I painted?'

'Walls.'

Of course. That was the only work he had seen me do, painting the house. No wonder his head teacher treated me rather condescendingly at the parents' evening later that month. It can be a salutary shock to see yourself as your children see you.

Worse was to come. I know now, from some of my own research, that we tend to put too much of the wrong sort of pressure on our children. We want them to be conventional successes from the beginning, even if the curriculum of their school does not fit their talents. Intelligence, I now know, thanks to Howard Gardner, is broader than IQ. You can be musically or athletically intelligent, and by music I don't necessarily mean the classical repertoire, and yet be hopeless in the rest of the curriculum. Pop musicians don't always or often get to university, nor do footballers, partly because their intelligence kicks in earlier. Being good with people, as our daughter was and is, as well as a brilliant organiser, does not count as much as those examination grades, even if helps more in life. So what do you do if your son turns out to be a gifted clarinet player, as ours did, winning a place in Britain's National Youth Orchestra at fifteen only to move on to be the saxophonist and lead singer of a pop group as soon as he left school, spending the next year in a succession of cellars playing and singing with his band? You can only encourage them, I thought, attend their gigs ('Please stand at the back, Dad, I don't want you to be too visible') and hope that it won't last, or, if it does, that he thrives.

It was strange to realise that the world they were entering was very different from the world I knew at their age, and that they were much more sure of what they wanted from life than I had been. It was also clear that our wishes for them were irrelevant, even counterproductive. When our son told us that he wanted to surrender his university place to go full time with his group and their manager ('As you know, Dad, it is getting into university that matters in this country, not going there') I told him, half seriously, that I was fully supportive of his decision if that was what he really wanted to do. Two weeks later he told me that the group had decided to disband and go to their respective universities as a better long-term bet. If I had tried to persuade him to give up the group he might, I suspect, have dumped the university just to assert his independence.

Sometimes, however, you feel that you can't win. One day I received a letter from our daughter that is still imprinted in my memory. I had been raising doubts about her choice of career. 'You have always,' she wrote, 'expected too much of your son and too little of me.' And I had only meant to take the pressure off her. Mostly, however, they survive those troublesome years of education and you are left wondering why you agonised so earnestly about the choice of school and endured those endless evenings where friends competed to boast of their offspring's scholastic or other successes. The awful truth slowly dawns that their real education was at home while you were busily engaged trying to live your own life. They watch and study you and then decide later to do the opposite or to imitate, and you can't be sure which is better because, most of the time, you were not modelling ideal behaviour.

Growing a family is never easy. Keeping the balance between the solidarity of the family and the individuality of its members demands sensitivity and compromise. Elizabeth uses her 'joiner' technique to capture this elusive balance in her portraits of families. In each portrait the family group takes centre stage, but included in the overall picture are individual images of each member. She asks each of them to pose with something that says something about them as a person, or to be doing something that expresses one of their enthusiasms. Initially, the younger members of the family are resistant even to the idea of a family portrait, but when they understand that they are able to pose as themselves, and not simply as sons or daughters, they become enthusiastic and involved.

It is the same balance that is at the heart of a relationship or of any group. Marriages work best when there is room for each to be separate as well as a bonded couple. My wife and I work closely together but it only succeeds because we do different things in different physical spaces. Anyone walking into our work areas would know at once that we have different ways of organising ourselves, different routines and different habits. We both cook, but I do it in the country, she in London. We do it differently, which adds spice to our mealtimes and takes the monotony out of it. We live together, but not too close together.

Some years before he died my father gave me a battered envelope. 'I won't ever get around to this now so you might as well have it.' The envelope contained our family tree, going back, supposedly, to the illegitimate daughter of Edward I. What intrigued me was how little indication there was of what my ancestors did – apart, that is, from the important fact that they had had offspring, because otherwise I would not be here. They were a vital part of the chain that ended up with me, and now with my two children. I was glad, then, that Elizabeth and I had kept the chain going. The Anglican marriage service has it about right, I thought, when it sets out the reasons why marriage was ordained – firstly for the procreation of children and their upbringing, secondly for legitimate sex (I am translating) and thirdly for 'the mutual society, help and comfort that the one ought to have of the other, both in prosperity and adversity.'

What has been exciting and rewarding in recent years is to see how that 'mutual society' has extended to include our children, who have not been children for many years now but more like companions, mentors even. In the new world they are wiser in many ways than us and touchingly concerned about our naivety in some areas and what they seem to feel is our increasing fragility. When your children become your friends you know that the family has worked.

In a world that sometimes seems to be fragmenting in every sphere, we all need somewhere to belong to as of right. Organisations won't do – they don't last long enough and are apt to cast one adrift when one's skills run out. Neighbours move on and lose touch. Too many relationships turn out to be shipboard romances – intense at the time but evanescent. The family, however, is always there even if it has to be dug out from time to time. Those who predict the decline of the family will be proved wrong. They may change their shape but they are not going to disappear. Families matter, but they do need nourishing. Communication is crucial. Suspicions and jealousies can grow wild in a silence. We take every opportunity we can to celebrate as a family, at weddings and festivals, big birthdays and anniversaries, even at funerals. Actually, any excuse for a big meal will do, on the basis that a family that eats well together will live long and well together.

I never imagined when I met Elizabeth that rainy night at a cocktail party in Kuala Lumpur that the result would one day be a new family, a family within a cluster of families in fact. My thoughts were much more short term, I'm afraid. Looking back now, all other parts of my life fade into insignificance by comparison. The family, all of it, is the best thing that has happened to me. Meantime, while our two children were busy launching themselves into their careers, I had my own to attend to.

Chapter Sixteen

Guru Times

Life sometimes unfolds in mysterious ways. Like the apocryphal butterfly in chaos theory that by fluttering its wings in China can precipitate a storm on the other side of the world, so, in our personal lives, far distant unrelated events can set things in motion that, in time, change our fortunes. So it was for me.

I had never heard of two McKinsey consultants called Tom Peters and Bob Waterman. Nor had most people. But, in 1982, the two of them published a book entitled *In Search of Excellence*. It put forward eight recipes for successful companies, with current examples of those companies that the authors believed to be following their precepts. It was readable, exciting, almost sexy, odd indeed for a business book. I was sent a copy of the American edition before it appeared in Britain and knew I had stumbled on a new kind of book. I secretly hoped that no one would get to hear about it in Britain because then I might purloin some of its idioms for my own teaching. It was not to be. The book was a huge best-seller around the world; my students came to class already armed with its messages.

It was not that it said anything very revolutionary. It was the way it said it, with recipes such as 'Stick to the Knitting', 'Be Close to the Customer', 'Tight-Loose Structure'. All of these are familiar business 'musts' today but were blindingly new concepts to many a manager at that time. What Peters and Waterman did was to take management theory out of the academic classroom into the public arena. Tom Peters went on to write many other books but he also took to the platform, enthralling audiences of managers around the world with electrifying, almost evangelistic, performances over two days, in which he entertained, provoked and challenged his listeners. He has described himself variously as gadfly, curmudgeon, champion of bold failures, prince of disorder, maestro of zest, corporate cheerleader and irritator. The self-descriptions give a taste of the man and his appeal. His books are stuffed with stories of real businesses and real people. The fact that many of the so-called 'excellent' companies cited in that first book later went off the rails does not diminish his enthusiasm or his appeal, although some quipped that to be mentioned in one of Tom's books was an omen of trouble ahead. Tom just says that they failed to keep to the maxims they helped him to create.

Tom Peters was the first management teacher to turn public performer in a serious way. *Fortune* called him the 'Ur-guru' or original guru. *The Economist* described him as the 'Ober-guru'. Peter Drucker had written more and for longer (he died aged ninety-five in 2005, writing to the end) and was probably the wisest of all, but he preferred to describe himself as a writer and was, in truth, a poor performer on a platform. Who first coined the word 'guru' to describe Peters and his like is unclear, and the word is not in any case particularly appropriate. Peter Drucker once quipped that journalists only came up with the word because 'charlatan' was too long for a headline. These management gurus do not cultivate groups of acolytes nor do they hold forth in any sort of management ashrams, but they do lay claim to certain truths about organisations and how they should be managed, and they are certainly not shy about their beliefs and ideas. There are now guru tables that rank the top fifty or so performers according to their popularity among managers, and there is a recognised core of people on the 'guru circuit' rather like professional tennis players. Some of these gurus reckon to do at least one hundred performances a year, usually at opera-star fees with the same sort of billing.

It is unclear how one comes to be a guru. You cannot apply to join the club, for there is in fact no formal club. Nor can you nominate yourself as a guru. It is a title that is given to you by the media or the speaker agencies that manage these folk. Most of them are American, because the circuit of conferences mostly exists in America, although it is now expanding alongside the spread of the global marketplace. By a nice piece of accidental timing Tom Peters and the guru phenomenon had really taken off when one of my books, *The Age of Unreason*, was published in America by the Harvard Business School Press in 1989. Tom very kindly provided a flattering blurb for the front cover, enveloping me in his aura. The book, luckily, struck a chord with some. Amongst other things, it foresaw the advent of the downsizing, outsourcing organisation that I christened the 'Shamrock Organisation' with its three leaves of the core employees, the subcontractors and the individual outside specialists or temporary workers. The point of using the shamrock metaphor was to emphasise that although the leaves were different categories of workers, they were also one leaf, part of one organisation, partners and allies, not subcontractors. Language shapes attitudes, I argued.

I was privately tickled to be approached at one conference in America by a group wearing T-shirts with shamrocks printed on them. 'We have renamed our business the Shamrock Corporation,' they said, 'because we are so persuaded by your ideas.' I wished them luck and hoped that they would not fall foul of the Tom Peters effect and crash too soon. As one result of the book I was approached by a speakers' bureau and signed up for an experimental year. It was a strange experience. I did not relish seeing myself in a catalogue, complete with photograph, along with thirty or so other speakers, offered as some sort of merchandise to anyone interested. Being part of a mail-order business in which I myself was the product was not my idea of my future. I resigned from their list after a year, but their catalogue had got my name into the guru club, even though most people assumed that I must be American.

Elizabeth became my official agent and the guardian of my image and reputation. She was by then, anyway, my personal photographer. No one else was ever allowed by her to take photos of me for public use. Together we laid down some rules for my speaking work. We agreed that we would only work with people whom we had first met personally, so that there could be some sort of relationship and trust. We would do a maximum of ten speaking engagements in a year, as long as they were with groups or in countries where I would meet new challenges, and only in the winter months. There would be five done for fees and five for expenses only, for deserving causes or projects, hoping that this would be enough to keep us solvent. The summer months had to be kept free for Elizabeth's photography.

I was determined both that these 'gigs', as they were called, should not take over our life and that I would learn from them. They were useful to me in that I met new people in new places, which was why I liked to stay for the whole event and, wherever possible, to spend a couple of days beforehand meeting relevant local people. They also provided a valuable test bed for new ideas for my books. These were the people I was writing for – if an idea didn't work in the conference hall or seminar I knew I had to rethink it.

As a result of our rules, each event, most of them abroad, might take up five to six days of our lives. Ten of those were quite enough. The real work was writing the books. I feared, however, that without the test beds of the gigs, my books might not have been either relevant or readable. Other authors send their manuscript around their friends and colleagues for comments. I used my audiences instead. 'You need not take notes,' I would tell them, 'it will be in a book one day soon.' I had learnt at Oxford to try to write as I speak because we had to read our essays out loud to our tutors. There is no way I had puff enough to read aloud a long sentence with a number of subordinate clauses. Keep those sentences short, I tell myself, not always successfully.

I also came across the 'fog index' in my early writing days. The fog index requires that you count all the words on a page and divide them by the number of full stops. That gives you the average sentence length. Then add one for every word of over three syllables and one for every technical term on that page. My pages tend to come out at a fog index of eighteen. The *Sun* newspaper averages under ten. *The Economist* is often over thirty. You have to gauge your audience, their attention span and their level of sophistication in your subject matter, but I doubt that you can hold the attention of a live audience, even if they are well versed in your topic, if you exceed a fog index of around twenty. Partly to keep my sentences under control I do not write my lectures or talks but speak directly to the audience without notes. That also allows me to have direct eye contact with them at all times. It does, however, require that I memorise my talk beforehand – a recipe for sleepless nights and some pre-performance nerves. 'It's easy for you,' my actor son says, 'you only have to learn your own lines. I have to learn Shakespeare's.'

'Yes,' I reply, 'but Shakespeare's lines scan, even rhyme at times, and none of his monologues are fifty minutes long.' You do have to be careful, however. The fog index dislikes words like 'imagination' or 'mellifluous' because of the number of syllables. Keep to it too religiously and you may screen out creativity, poetry and beauty.

The guru thing added interest and excitement and travel to our lives throughout my sixties. Like much of the rest of my life I was a slow starter. When my contemporaries were thinking of retirement I found myself busier than ever. Luckily, age seems irrelevant in the guru world. It is the ideas and their presentation that matter. That is also true of ever more occupations as people move into the knowledge and information economies. Your piano tuner may be blind and over eighty, but if his hearing is still good and his fingers work you don't care; whether the piano is in tune is the only question that matters. The same is true of anyone in the creative world. Talent is non-ageist, colour-blind and unaware of disabilities. I keep on my desk a copy of Lucien Freud's self-portrait, painted when he was eighty; just to remind me that it is the work, not the age, that counts, the art in his case, the ideas, and how they are expressed, in mine.

What ideas? If I am strictly honest, few of my ideas are that original. It is the words I use that make the difference. I still treasure the review that I read of my first book. 'There is nothing in this book,' it started, 'that has not been said before.' My heart sank. Then it went on, 'But it has probably never been read before.' He had perfectly captured my intent in that first book in which I was revamping the known research on organisations in language that would mean more to my students.

At that time, back in 1976, it was the academic language of the research studies, mostly from America, that was baffling. Today it is the language that organisations have invented for themselves that is pretentious, unrelated to what actually happens on the ground and often devoid of real meaning. All professions and occupations invent their own codes and technical terms. It is functionally effective even if it also locks out those who haven't learnt the language that the professionals use. Management has, however, often gone over the top in its exaggerated language, which has either become a cliché, meaning nothing much anymore, or is so gobbledegook that only a few initiates can decipher it, and you can't run organisations with a few initiates. Examples are widespread. Every organisation claims that they care deeply for its customers, is even passionate about them, although you might be dubious if you are still trying to get through to their helpline after forty minutes. Every organisation proclaims that their employees are their most precious asset, even while making swathes of them redundant. All businesses have a strategic development plan, which, more often than not, is just a hoped-for projection of the present. Every business is committed to excellence and to aiming for world-class, even though research suggests that only a tiny few achieve it. As a result these terms have ceased to mean anything distinctive. They are the new clichés of management.

Then there are the new terms that the professionals of management, the consultants and business schools and even a few of the gurus have introduced: Re-engineering, Core Competences, JIT, Six Sigma, 360-degree Feedback, CRM, Social Network Analysis, Globalisation, Format Competition and ROI Marketing are just some of the pseudo-technical terms that make the obvious seem clever. One bank is currently claiming to 'leverage its global footprint to provide effective financial solutions for its customers by providing a gateway to diverse markets'. I assume that it is just saying it is there to help its customers wherever they are. Such pseudo language creates a false mystique, suggesting that there are technical or professional answers to every management problem.

The reality, I believe, is very different, and much simpler. Organisations are not machines that can be neatly designed, mapped, measured and controlled. The fact that some particular operations can be and have to be managed in that way has deceived people into thinking that the whole organisation is just one super-project. That is what logicians call a category error. For too long management theorists appropriated the language of engineering to describe the way organisations worked. People were human resources, things that could be costed, allocated, controlled and shunted around as the need arose; they were managed, in short. In everyday language it is things that are managed, not people. It is sensible to speak of managing the audio-visual equipment, but not to lump the technicians in with it.

The word is intrinsically confusing. We say 'manage' when we often mean just 'coping'. When you say to your spouse 'How did you manage today?' you are not expecting in reply a discourse on motivation theory. 'Manage' can even mean getting around to doing something, as in 'Did you manage to fix the car?' In using the language of things and machines to get a grip on their organisations, managers have unintentionally made their jobs more difficult. People do not like being seen as things, nor as problems to be coped with or got around to. If the words we use don't mean what we want them to mean it is better to change the language than to redefine the words. We are not in *Alice in Wonderland* where words can be made to mean anything we want them to. In the real world twisting words only confuses the listeners. Organisations are not machines. That has been the central message of all my books. They are living communities of individuals. To describe them we need to use the language of communities and the language of individuals. That means a mix of the words we use in politics and in ordinary everyday life. The essential task of leadership (a word from political theory, unlike the word 'manager') is to combine the aspirations and needs of the individuals with the purposes of the larger community to which they all belong.

You do not need to be a genius to see that the task is much easier if the leader knows what the purpose of the community should be and can convince everyone of its importance. The individuals in the community must also be the right ones for the different tasks. In general, if people know what they have to do and why, if they have the skills to do it, are trusted to get on with it as best they can and are appropriately rewarded when they succeed, the community will be more likely to succeed in its mission. It is all, of course, much easier to say than to do, but it does not make the task any easier to dress it up in fancy language or acronyms.

My belief is that most people have a fundamental understanding of what makes organisations work. They just need to be reminded of it and encouraged to apply their understanding to their own work. The late Sumantra Goshal of the London Business School once described Peter Drucker as practising the scholarship of common sense. I would like that to be said of me. For example, it is only common sense that people are more likely to be committed to a cause or mission if they have had a hand in shaping it. That does not need research to prove it. Nor do you have to see the research to know that groups are likely to produce better results than the same individuals acting on their own. Teams of all-stars are not always or even often the best teams. The egos get in the way of the sharing. The film *True Blue*, based on the Oxford rowing team that dumped its international oarsmen because of their arrogant intransigence, replaced them with the second crew and went on to win the Boat Race against Cambridge, was a vivid example of this. We all have different talents and personalities. Put the right people with the right companions and everything clicks; get it wrong and there can be chaos. That is only common sense, even if it is uncommon in practice.

Above all people know instinctively that there has to be trust if any organisation is going to work; trust between those in the group, that they will do their best and won't undermine you, as well as trust in their leaders. People implicitly understand that the trust involved has to be earned and can't be assumed, that it depends as much on who you are as on what you do, that it is fragile and, once lost, can seldom be restored. They also know that it is hard to rely on people you don't know, or whom you only contact electronically. Elaborate research studies are not needed to demonstrate such a basic truth. Yet organisations need trust if they are not going to clutter themselves up with rules, checks and checkers. Too much time is spent in organisations making sure that what should have happened is happening. If people know what they have to do and are competent to do it, they should be left alone to get on with it.

I often ask executives to list the people they know well enough and long enough to be able to rely on them to do the right thing when they themselves are not around and trouble is brewing. They seldom come up with more than twenty names. That suggests that, to be truly efficient and also effective, organisations should be designed around operational units of less than twenty. On paper, that looks wasteful. Organisations inevitably tidy up the design, optimistically hoping that the economic logic of scale will prevail over the psychological need for trust and human intimacy and that everyone will do their best to make the place work. They are then surprised to be disappointed. It is a particular difficulty for large organisations whose very existence is often based on those economies of scale. Could they have both, then, for both are necessary? Can you combine big and small? The answer, from political theory, is yes. Federalism is a well-tested way of doing just that, and there are clear principles, tested over time, of how federalism works. We could read the *Federalist Papers*, that intellectual foundation of the American constitution, for a start. What we have to do is to apply those principles to organisations.

One of my other beliefs is that we don't need to reinvent a theory of organisations. As more and more organisations are dependent on the skills of their people, they are having to treat those people, even those at the lower ends of the organisation, as professionals, people with recognised skills and talents. We should therefore look at the way we have traditionally run professional organisations to see what messages we can learn from these centuries-old institutions.

Go to the theatre, I say to my readers and listeners. Look first at the programme as you wait for the curtain to rise. Everyone connected with the performance is listed, no matter how small their contribution. People like to be recognised as individuals. Theatre companies don't talk of their actors as human resources – none of them would work for them if they did. Look more closely at that programme. The word 'manager' is reserved for those in charge of things, not people, the stage manager, the lighting manager. Nor are the names of these managerial people in large type; that distinction goes to the people who are in direct communication with the customer, the actors, and they are directed, not managed, by someone who actually leaves the scene once the project is under way. He or she trusts the cast to go it alone and, as often as not, they improve on the production once the director departs. Trust inspires. One more thing – at the end of each performance they receive an expression of appreciation from their audience, direct feedback from the people who matter. No waiting for the annual performance appraisal.

The lessons are all there for those who care to look. In professional and service organisations it is the person who is in direct contact with the client who is most responsible for the first and often lasting impressions that are formed of the organisation. That may be the person in the call centre, the engineer who comes to repair the machine, the sales assistant behind the counter, even the waiter at your table. Paradoxically, however, it is often the people in front of the customer who are the worst paid. That does not make the task of management easy. How believable is it to say you are crucial to our business, when the pay packet tells a different story? In a ritual genuflection to the importance of individuality, organisations try to compensate a little by requiring such people to display their name. It fools no one, neither the worker nor the customer.

Because organisations are collections of ordinary humans, I like to think that we can draw the necessary lessons from our own everyday lives. The way we learn, the way we relate to the people we need, or to those we have to live with, these can all provide lessons for the worlds we work in. Life is life whether in the family or the office. At first I used to draw my stories from a variety of business case studies, but I discovered that people found it easier to relate to stories from ordinary life than from organisations they had never encountered. It is then my task to show how they apply to the world of work.

I am also convinced that people find it easier to remember images than concepts, that pictures live longer in the mind than technical terms. I like to lard my talks with pictures, often photographs taken by Elizabeth or copies of works of art. Great art, I find, is great, at least in part, because it deals so pungently with a human dilemma or expresses some dimension of our human condition. Rachel Whiteread's sculptures, which model in cement or plastic the insides and undersides of familiar objects such as chairs or staircases, make visible the bits of our environment that we don't see or notice. They remind me to look under the surface of things to glimpse what is there but ignored by most, like those in-front-of-the-customer staff. The clues to our future also lie, I often think, in what is already happening but is going unnoticed, such as the rise of the independent or free agent economy, or the move from ownership to rights in company law. Innovation, too, I suggest to my listeners, can spring from seeing the unnoticed space beneath the stairs before anyone else.

Good stories and good metaphors can also conjure up images in people's minds. The shamrock was an early metaphor. The sigmoid curves, those two curves of life and change, were another, providing a visual image of a human dilemma. Doughnuts, too, I tell my puzzled audiences, can hold the key to designing an effective organisation. The jam in any job, the bit at the centre of the doughnut, represents the tasks that have to be done, the dough is the space for initiatives. Doughnuts that are all jam and no dough give the person or group no responsibility for any initiative. Too much dough and too little jam in the middle and the organisation will have no control over the core task. Large doughnuts, however, require a clear sense of the mission of the organisation and a shared passion for delivering it. Otherwise the space for initiatives could be misused, leading to that space being steadily reduced with a resulting loss of motivation. Targets without the room for initiative are doughnuts without the dough. They won't work. The doughnut, therefore, is a graphic way of looking at appropriate delegation. A federal organisation is, in essence, a large doughnut made up of mini doughnuts. Get the doughnuts right, with the proper balance between the core and the space for freedom, and the whole should gel. I have even used the doughnut to describe the dilemmas of modern capitalism – too much jam for too few and too many left in the dough.

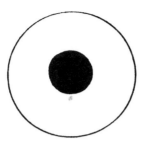

Shamrocks, doughnuts, rowing eights and portfolios are examples of my attempt to translate conceptual ideas into memorable images. They are what I regard as low-definition ideas. They are not precisely definable, they don't tell you what to do, they are intended to stimulate thought not to substitute for it. My aim is to interpret people's worlds for them, not to tell them how to deal with it. It would, I feel, insult their intelligence and independence were I to imply that I knew better how to live their lives or run their organisations than they did. But if I can help them to understand their situation better, I may have allowed them to see more clearly what risks and opportunities lie before them.

More and more, however, I have moved from dealing with the 'how' questions to the 'why' ones. It is the Socratic impulse that keeps me questioning. Why do we need such big organisations, when most of us don't relish working in them? Why do we treat those within them in the ways that we do? Why do we live our lives as we do? Success has many faces. Why do we choose the ones we do? Why do we all agree on so many of the injustices of the world but do nothing about them? Why do we continue to cling to gods that have failed us? Is there too much love of money, for its own sake? Or is capitalism at fault – or, more truthfully, our interpretation of capitalism?

I can't, I tell my executive audiences and readers, think of any better mechanism for making the world a better place than a set of open-market economies, carefully regulated so that they remain properly competitive. But it is the phrase 'making the world a better place' that is often missing from the capitalist narrative. As it is currently seen and measured, capitalism takes selfishness to be its driving force, something that can easily develop into greed. Capitalism assumes that it is part of the human condition to be all out for ourselves in a dog-eat-dog world. We are hard-wired for competition. It is a rather dismal assumption. Nor is it necessarily a true one. There is an altruistic gene in most of us. Most of us want to contribute to as well as take from the world. The danger, as I see it, is that the language of capitalism, reinforced by its instruments and the measures they use, may imprison us in a cause that we don't necessarily believe in. But, when the more brutalist version of capitalism is dominant what else can most of us do except conform to the stereotype, muttering dissent as we go?

Because the capitalist narrative decrees that more is better, businesses continually buy their competitors, and are aided and abetted by their bankers and consultants in so doing, although all the evidence is that only in a minority of cases does the end result leave the customer or the purchasing shareholders better off. Why, then, do they continue to do it, creating organisations too big for human scale in the process? Why do organisations, when reporting their actions during the year, speak only of results for them, seldom for their customers or the world at large? Because, I have to assume, more is thought to be better, be it more power, bigger sales or greater influence. Yet we know that in much of the rest of life, and in other organisations, more is not always better. I sometimes suggest to business executives that if they were to ask a symphony orchestra what its growth plans were for the coming year, they might not speak of increasing the number of musicians, or even the number of performances, but would talk more of growing their repertoire and their reputation. Yes, more money would help, but only as a means to achieve those ends. It is no different for other arts organisations, or schools, better often when smaller. Meeting with a wine grower in the Napa Valley who told me that his ambition was to grow his business, I said, looking around me, 'Where will you find the extra land, or are you going to buy up your neighbours?'

'Oh, I don't need to grow bigger,' he replied, 'just better.'

Why don't more businesses think like that, I wonder?

Business, I continue to argue, mistakes its means for its ends, and will always continue to do so until we, society backed by government, redefine those ends to make them more relevant to the needs of more people. It is not enough, I believe, to pay one's taxes and leave the rest to government.

Inevitably, perhaps, my messages are a reflection of my values. I do care more for individuals than organisations, who are, after all, just their instruments. I believe that if organisations were to take more seriously the individuals who are, in effect, the organisation, they would find their own objectives easier to achieve. I believe that organisations are, in a broad sense, the servants of society. They exist to provide us with the things and services we need or want. We rely on them to do so efficiently and effectively. Ideally, their interests and ours should coincide, but they will prosper most if they define their purpose as something bigger than their own survival. Those organisations, as well as those individuals, who work only for their own benefit, eventually discover that they are their own worst customer, because they are never satisfied, seldom thanked and leave no legacy. The definition of success in our modern affluent world is one of our more intractable problems. It was easier once when we had fewer choices. Now we can choose but have no good criterion for the choices. Even business executives have to be philosophers.

Chapter Seventeen
Travels with a Microphone

Would I be interested in offering a management seminar to the local
business people in Calcutta, now Kolkata? It was the British Council
enquiring, hearing that I might be passing through India en route to
Australia. The British Council is an admirable institution staffed with
splendid people, but they are not rich. The fee they offered was minimal.
But my agent, Elizabeth, is nothing if not imaginative. 'Pay him
nothing,' she said, 'but you must have all the right connections, so
could you arrange for us to have an hour alone with each of the four
most interesting people in Calcutta?'

So it was that we met privately and personally with the chief minister,
who turned out to be a jovial Marxist, with Mother Teresa, surrounded
by her nuns, the vice-chancellor of the university and a prominent local
artist. Money can't buy that sort of experience. The pattern was set.
We have made the same sort of contract in various countries around
the world, where our hosts have contacts and influence but little money.
Sometimes it is private dinners and lunches that they arrange with
politicians and leading citizens, sometimes visits to local businesses,
schools, or museums and opera houses, to meet the people who run
them. Not only does it allow me to make my talks or seminars more
relevant, it is a fun way to learn about the world and its differing
complexions.

The truth is that I am not a very good tourist. I don't much enjoy
looking at famous sights or crawling around ruins, just to say that I

have been there, or to store images away in my memory bank. To be more accurate I am what you might call a sociological tourist, I like to observe how a country works, how its people live and work and, if possible, to meet them. The best way to do that, without being an intrusive voyeur, is to have some work to do in the places you want to visit. I've been fortunate – there have been enough invitations down the years to give lectures or seminars in different corners of the world to keep my curiosity sated, with hosts that seem only too ready to share their contacts with us in return.

The best tourist aid of all, however, is a BBC microphone. Thanks to an enterprising and talented producer, I have been privileged to make a number of radio programmes for the BBC. Most people are only too pleased to talk into a microphone with those magic letters, BBC, on top of it, as long as they know you are not conspiring against them. In one series I was asked to revisit my life's journey to explore my own religious quest for the meaning of life. I went back to the Ireland of my birth, to Oxford, Singapore, America, Windsor and Tuscany, to meet people who lived there now and to reflect on what it had been like in my times there and what I had learnt about God and life. It was a fascinating opportunity, one given to few, to be able to retalk and rewalk your life in this way and to see how the world had changed while you were away.

Amongst other things, I realised, to my embarrassment, how naive I had been in my youth, how little I had done with my time in some of those places, how long it had taken me to grow up, to be less concerned with how I was doing and instead to take an interest in those around me. I remember standing on the padang in Kuala Lumpur on Merdeka Day in 1957 when the Union Jack was lowered for the last time and the Malayan one raised in its place, to mark the granting of independence to that bit of the old British Empire. But I also remember being more interested in wondering when I would be able to get a beer than in the feelings of the newly independent citizens around me.

You have to listen if it's a microphone you are carrying for others to talk into. And each time, in each place, you feel for a while that the world revolves around the place where you are standing. For the people you are meeting their place is indeed the centre of the world as they look at it. It is salutary to find no news at all of things European, let alone British, in the Ugandan newspapers, not even when the Live Aid concerts were playing in London. In New Zealand they take a quiet pleasure from the maps that put New Zealand at the centre of the globe with Britain a small blob at the top edge. When, a week or so later, I return to my own centre, in the fields of East Anglia in Britain, I find it hard to remember that life is still going on in the city I have just left thousands of miles away. It takes a major disaster like a tsunami, an earthquake or a famine, and a media blitz, to jolt us out of our own world. Ten days later we forget again. I am one of those news addicts, bereft without my daily paper, partly because it reminds me that there is a wider world, beyond the horizons I can see.

That's one more reason why we travel, to remind us that there are many centres in the world, each important to those who live there, people whose concerns are very like ours – living, loving, learning and hoping to leave a legacy – but whose circumstances can be very different. The tea picker in Darjeeling, for instance, so proud of his family as Elizabeth photographed them on one of our trips, but stern and unsmiling. What would become of his children, we wondered, and he wondered too, probably. He wanted a better life for them than the gruelling days under the sun plucking tiny leaves from the bushes to fill the bag on the back. The tea company had built a nice school, free for all the children of the tea workers, and was teaching them to read and write and count. It might make it possible for them to go off to a bigger school in the town and later to college in faraway Delhi. But would life in the big city really be better than the village life of their parents?

It was the old question of progress again. Is more better? Can we ever stop the world, our world, where it is, or do we always have to keep trying to move it onward? What will happen to those idyllic tea gardens, those rolling waves of green camellia bushes under the umbrellas of the shade trees, if the children of the current tea pickers go off to college? Will they mechanise the gardens, driving huge machines through the bushes? Already they have a factory turning the leaves into powder for instant tea. It looks like a small refinery, all pipes and columns. It's what the market wants, they say. It's progress – of a sort.

You have to wonder. The market does have an inexorable force. It is hard to hide from it, hard to avoid competition. If you don't go along with it, others will in some other part of the world, selling to your customers. That's globalisation for you, a world with no place to hide. The lovely hand-picked, hand-sorted Darjeeling tea, the sort where the leaves stick to the edge of the cup, is a rare thing now, and pricey. We treasure our annual Christmas gift from the tea gardens, but reflect, as we taste it, how most tea, like so many things, is now a commodity. Who knows where it comes from or how it is picked? Or how much those pickers are paid. Who cares? In spite of the best efforts of the Fair Trade campaigners and others like them, busy shoppers just buy tea. The market pushes everything towards a common denominator, into a world of same things. Efficient, but sad. Differences do delight.

It's because of the differences that I like most the small countries, countries that, like my own Ireland, have small populations. Countries like Uganda, Singapore, New Zealand, Slovenia, or the Baltic countries, Estonia, Latvia and Lithuania. It is easier to get my head around their situations. I call them flea economies, as opposed to the elephant countries that dominate international trade. It is their differences that fascinate, differences that they are keen to preserve as one bulwark against the cloning forces of that global market. Most of them have nothing except their agricultural land and the talents of their people. Singapore does not even have any land but, per capita, it is one of the richest countries in the world. So is Ireland, but only in the last few years. Watch out for Slovenia and Estonia, but don't count on Uganda joining them. Will New Zealand make it to the top league or not? Why are they each so different? What can I learn from them in my journeys?

I can learn a bit of economics, for a start. My hypothesis is that flea economies do very well if they can in some way ride on the back of a major elephant. Ireland benefited hugely from her membership in the European Union. It wasn't just the subsidies and grants that she received as she moved out of the developing-country stage. The enticements that the Irish government offered to foreign firms, mainly American, to locate there, also helped. They used Ireland as their jumping-off place for the European market, helped by the common language and a well-educated, young and, for a while, cheap labour force.

With the help of these imported businesses Ireland moved from an agricultural economy to a knowledge and information economy without going through the smokestacks of the old industrial age. The young Irish took to the new world with enthusiasm. In a league table of internationalisation compiled by the consultants A. T. Kearney, Ireland comes top by a mile, with not only a larger proportion of imports and exports, but also registering more foreign travel per capita, and more international phone calls. Europe has been good for Ireland, but Ireland was well prepared for it, having invested in higher and technical education two decades earlier and having set out to woo international firms at the same time. Once the firms started to appear the Irish saw the sense in getting an education, particularly in technology. So was the Celtic tiger born.

New Zealand has the same population as Ireland and, like Ireland, for a long time was tied into and dependent on the British market, a useful although remote elephant. With the end of the advantages that imperial protection used to give her and which had to be abandoned when Britain entered the Common Market, New Zealand was left without an elephant to lean on and to sell into. She needs to find a new one. Australia is not big enough and America is too far away. So, most of New Zealanders feel, is China. Meantime, with the dwindling exception of her agricultural exports, she has to make do with her home market, which is too small to allow her small firms to grow big enough to be world-class competitors.

New Zealand, however, is a relaxed society, far removed physically from the crises of the rest of the world, with an adequate standard of living. There is a sense among much of the population that it would be a shame to have to work so hard that you miss out on the other sides of life. Visiting our daughter who lived there for six years, I watched the local plumber come to repair her shower one morning. While he was working his phone rang. Clearly, he was wanted somewhere else, urgently, as is the way with plumbers. His crisis wasn't quite what I expected. He put down the phone, turned to my daughter and said, 'Sorry I've got to run. The surf's running. But I'll be back in two hours.' My daughter was unfazed. It clearly happened all the time in her seaside town.

Perhaps the Kiwis are right. Life is about more than economics, particularly when you live in a beautiful land with empty roads and beaches. But to maintain public services at levels comparable to the rest of the world, the economy has to grow. A global world invites comparisons. No one can afford to fall too far behind or their best citizens may leave. Economic growth is a relentless treadmill that no one dare step off. One day those Kiwis will need their own elephant companies and an elephant country to sell into.

A joined-up world is a restless place, one where it is unwise for a country to stand still, where each success seems to be only the prelude to yet another problem and, worst of all, where it is unclear where the road leads to in the end, if, indeed, there is an end. The journey may well not be worth all the hassle, progress might be an illusion, but there seems to be no alternative anywhere but to keep travelling. Like all of life, I suppose. Why should countries be different from us?

Globalisation is at best a mixed blessing. For one thing, no one can opt out of it, not even tiny Bhutan, which is gradually being compelled to open up its closed society. There can be no rest anywhere now. But, yes, it does encourage, even force, the spread of technology as companies and countries fight to keep up. The relentless search for competitive advantage keeps the busy capitalist bees on an endless search for the newest and cheapest nectar. That drives the costs and the prices down but it also leads the bees to move to ever newer territories, spreading their know-how wider and bringing jobs and wealth in their train. That is the good news. The bad news is that when they move on they leave a vacuum behind them, unless the territories they leave have been able to use the injection of money and expertise to build their own talent bank and to hold it within their borders.

Global capitalism is inherently greedy and in a hurry. Countries think in generations, corporations in years, five at most. Well meaning though most of them are, they have what the sociologist Erving Goffman once called 'taxicab' relationships with their host countries, intimate but short. Their hosts have to make the most of them while they are around, and put up with some of the dislocations they may cause, but, first, they have to tempt them to come in. Unfortunately, one of those dislocations is the seemingly inevitable consequence of economic growth. The faster an economy grows the bigger becomes the gap between the income of those at the top and those at the bottom, even when, as in Britain, there is a Labour-government pledge to reduce it. Sadly, it seems that as the gap grows so does the propensity to bad health, depression and violence among those left behind. Paradoxically, economic growth often brings social decline in its wake. Nothing is easy.

That growing income gap can be traced back to the global market-place where talent and labour, like everything else, is traded across national boundaries, so that the price for the best talent is fixed internationally, as is the cost of labour at the other end. The market simultaneously and perversely forces costs down and some prices up. The winner takes all, as one book title has it. So the rich get richer and the poor, even though they may get richer in absolute terms, are left further behind. It is not clear to me how the trend can be reversed, although we can, of course, do more to raise the floor, and make absolute poverty history by bringing the poorest into that market economy. It would be in our own interests. In the end, if the rich are to go on getting richer they will have to help the poor to get richer first so that the whole world economy can grow exponentially. Odd, isn't it, that the international marketplace that causes much of the problem should also be the best way to solve it? But that's economics for you.

My travels with a microphone left me feeling guilty. I felt like a voyeur, looking in on other people's lives but doing nothing to help. I was myself largely untouched by the predicaments of the lands we visited. It was different on one journey. We visited South Africa in the months immediately following the release of Nelson Mandela and the build-up to the first truly free elections in that country. I was due to address a large personnel conference and our hosts had kindly arranged for us to meet some trade union leaders and members of the ANC. To a man, they refused to condemn the previous regime or even to talk about it. Their gaze was fixed firmly on the future. The Truth and Reconciliation Commission that later followed was a wonderful way for people to expunge their guilt while accepting responsibility for their misdeeds. I realised, once again, that a nation can't move forward unless it accepts the past and puts it behind it, that if it can't face up to the truth about itself it will be stuck with the old problems. Ireland, I reflected, didn't begin to move until it stopped lamenting the troubles of the past, forgave its supposed oppressors and took responsibility for its own destiny. That is as true for individuals as it is for countries, and just as difficult. I left South Africa impressed and hopeful for their people, despite all their difficulties, and resolved, personally, to learn from their example.

Chapter Eighteen
A Seventieth Birthday

I woke early on 25 July three years ago in what was still our apartment in Tuscany. I groaned as I realised what day it was. Suddenly, in one instant of time I had become seventy years old. The fateful bar had been crossed, the biblical span of life completed. My close family had gathered to celebrate the event. What exactly were we celebrating, I wondered? Survival, I guessed. Improbably for Tuscany in late July it was raining outside, I noticed. Was this an omen?

I looked in the mirror. That was definitely an old face. Did it belong to me? I did not feel that way. A few weeks before, on the Tube in London, a beautiful elegant young Ethiopian – or was she Sudanese? – lady had caught my eye and smiled. 'Ah!' I thought, 'thank goodness, I've still got some of the old spark left, it seems.' Then I realised that she was offering me her seat. Blushing, I accepted, trying not to show how disappointed I was. I comforted myself that eighty was the new seventy, that there might still, with luck and good health, be another ten years before I was really old. After all, I was still playing tennis, albeit badly, still swimming every morning, still cycling, walking, drinking too much red wine, still working full time.

But the signs were there, I recognised. The back creaked if I tested it too much. It was stiff in the early mornings. I found it easier to sit down to put on my socks. I was taking pills for this and that each morning. Daily reminders of my mortality. I suppose I was lucky that there weren't more of them.

Death itself was now something within my planning horizon. It had finally entered my generation. The death of parents, aunts and uncles is upsetting but to be expected if they happen in the fullness of their time. It is when your contemporaries start to die that you wake up, start to read the obituaries with a new interest, checking first to see how old they were. We go to more funerals and memorials these days, always sad but also, in a strange way, reflective and almost enjoyable, so many familiar faces with so many reminiscences to share, the sadness often relieved by the thought of a life well lived. I go away, however, realising that my own time can't be that far off. Time to put my house in order, I say to myself. Then optimism takes over. Plan to live forever, they say, but live each day as if it were your last. Good advice of course, but hard to live up to when the days are sometimes cloudy.

But will those who come to my funeral think my own life well lived, I also ask myself? I have been privileged, down the years, to be given honorary doctorates by a number of universities. On these occasions one usually has to stand on the platform in front of all the newly grad-uated students while a member of the faculty reads out the citation, or justification, for the award of your degree. It feels like an advance obituary. I have often stood there wondering if I am already dead. They are always complimentary, these citations. They have to be. You don't criticise the person you are honouring. So they are only part of the truth of who we are. Our real lives are usually concealed from the public gaze. Even those who court the public and the paparazzi seldom reveal their full selves. We, who should know ourselves best, are not always prepared to face the truth, but, as death edges nearer, there is less to lose in being honest with yourself about the sort of life you have lived.

Aristotle advised us to take the deathbed test, to imagine ourselves on our last day in life and to consider how we should evaluate our lives. At times I have asked executives in a seminar to take a version of this test. 'Imagine yourself dying at a ripe old age. Write the short eulogy you would like your best friend to deliver for you at a memorial ceremony.' They find it difficult, of course, because they are still in the midst of their working careers. Indeed, those who are under thirty and have not yet been close to death or seen any of their nearest and dearest die, are unable to contemplate such a situation and turn it into a fantasy or joke. When the older ones do complete the exercise they have to imagine themselves standing at the end of their life, aged perhaps eighty. If they can look back from there, they realise that much of what currently consumes their time and energy will be insignificant in the longer view of their life. Their imagined friend in his or her eulogy would probably skate over the details of their career to focus on what kind of person they had been, put in a reminiscence or two and end with the memories they will leave behind for those who knew them best. Who they were will often matter more than what they did.

I did the exercise once myself, in my fifties. It persuaded me that to spend my time creating a CV that would impress strangers would be a waste of time in the end. Already I knew that the achievements, such as they were, of my earlier career had been swallowed up in the wastes of the passing years. Organisations have bad memories and quickly forget your once familiar face and name. There are few more salutary lessons than to return to places where your word had once held sway and your name mattered, only to find that no one knew who you were, recognised the name or the face. 'I was the chairman here once,' I found myself saying to the receptionist. 'Oh, really?' was the only response. *Sic transit gloria mundi.*

So what do I want to leave behind, and for whom? What personal legacy? Not my talks or broadcasts. I know the research on mental retention. I know, sadly, that eighty per cent of anything I said would have gone from the minds of those who listened before they even left the room or turned off the radio. Not my books. I have shelves of them, copies of each edition in many different languages. I keep them only for reference and as nostalgic reminders of times past. I have requested that they all be ritually burnt after my death. They can also throw on all those scrolls recording the honorary degrees or other awards. They are only the detritus of a life. I rather fancy the notion of a pyre in the field behind my house with my family standing around as my life's work burns – the nearest I can get to an Indian funeral in Britain. If the ideas in those books had any value they will by then be absorbed into other people's ways of thinking. That would be something I could be proud of, even though I could never know which idea had connected with whom.

Forget the CV then, so arduously put together over the years. Forget the books. Forget the physical me. I shall be rotting in the earth. The idea of NOTHING for afters does not worry me. If I have never given a thought to what existed before I existed why should I care about anything afterwards? What I hope will endure for a time with those I hold most dear, my family and a few close friends, is some memory of me as a person. If there is any kind of immortality it lies in the minds and hearts of others. I find that I think and dream of my own parents, dead now for a quarter of a century, more than I ever did when they were alive. Which is rather shocking really, when I think about it.

There is a Jewish tradition of the living will in which you formally bequeath to your heirs, apart from any physical objects or money, your beliefs and values, in the hope that they may carry them on into their own lives. I could not be so presumptuous as to prescribe how others should live, but I have written letters to my wife and two children, letters to be opened after my death, letters in which I spell out my hopes for each of them as well as just a few words on what I have found to matter most in my life. I update them each year. If I am honest they are more for my benefit than theirs, forcing me to focus my thoughts. It is my version of Aristotle's deathbed exercise. I never knew what my father felt about life, or about death. I wish I had.

My family tease me that I am, like T. S. Eliot's Webster, much possessed by death. That is because, like Aristotle, I think that you can only really assess your life at the end of it. In anticipating the end of my life I am setting myself the goal of living up to my imagined eulogy in the time that remains. By the time most of us are ready to do that we are on our literal deathbed, not the imagined one. It is always tempting to postpone the inventory of our lives for just a little longer, while we get on with living them. Self-knowledge can be a bitter medicine. In most tragedies the protagonist leaves it too late. When Faust finally saw the error of his ways it was too late, he was dead.

The deathbed discipline helps to keep me focused on what really matters, even if, like most of us, I don't always manage to keep to my resolutions. The good news is that it gets easier as one gets older. Ambition fades, as does the envy of others who are ostensibly more successful. That's mostly because the opportunities have long passed and because, by then, we have rationalised our past and any of its failures in order to allow ourselves to live comfortably with it. I have noticed that when well-known people are asked to reflect on their worst mistake for some newspaper profile they always end up seeing it as an important learning experience that, in hindsight, they are pleased to have had. It may even have been one of those triggers that set them off in a new direction and became a turning point in their lives.

As age progresses, there are also fewer people left whom one might want to impress. So one might as well speak the truth as one sees it, live as one wants to, spend time with only those one values. St Augustine saw life as a ladder of temptations, a ladder you climbed by treading on each in turn, crushing them as you stepped higher. Unlike most climbs this one seems to get lighter with age and progress, most of the temptations long ago stamped out.

Lying there on my birthday morning there were things that I wished had been different in my life. I would rather not have spent all my twenties trying to be an oil executive. On the other hand, and there is always another hand, I would not then have experienced a great organisation from the inside, I would not have enjoyed the delights of South-

East Asia before it was overrun by tourists like me. Crucially, I would not have met Elizabeth. I remembered my mother saying farewell to me as I departed for Malaysia for three long years. 'Don't worry, dear,' she said, 'it will be good material for your books.'

'Books?' I said, puzzled, 'I'm going to be an oil man, not a writer.' Mothers sometimes know us better than we know ourselves. Yes, in retrospect she was right. I should not regret those years.

I regret, just sometimes, that I was already married and properly domesticated by the time the swinging sixties came along and never got to enjoy their alleged freedoms. I would have liked more money, too, in the early years of our marriage, but I was not prepared to do what was necessary to earn it. I would have enjoyed being on the inner track of some part of the political process, able in some way to influence the choices made by governments, but was not ready to sell my soul, or even my time, to any political party. Nothing comes without cost and I was not prepared to face the cost.

I would like to have my youth over again. I didn't do enough in those precious years. Ireland was a dull land then and I was a dull lad. I didn't travel, didn't do sports, didn't take enough interest in the natural world around me. On the other hand, balancing my memories once again, I did read a lot in those dull days. Perhaps in old age that is a more useful pastime. Less selfishly, I regret, now, that I never got my hands dirty, that I never worked with the poor or the unemployed, only wrote about them. I have never campaigned on the streets, never joined a protest march. In my voyeurish treks I have been to some of the poorest parts of the world but have never stayed behind to help. It is best to do these things when you are young, full of energy and less concerned about where you will be sleeping and what the bathroom facilities are like, but I was too concerned with my own future then, not anyone else's. Even today, while I write cheques to some good causes, I keep my own hands clean. I argue, possibly correctly, that these days I would be more a nuisance than a help.

Perhaps that was always true. I remembered again the words of the bishop who advised me not to get ordained. 'Stay where you are,' he said, 'do what you are doing. You have the access to the kind of people that most priests never meet. Use it to do good in any way you can.' It was my escape clause, and I have used it ever since as my reason for sticking to what I know. He may well have been right, but the guilt of my clean hands that I carry over from my youth in the vicarage still pricks.

Aristotle would have agreed with the bishop, I believe. Do your best with what you are best at, is my translation of his principle of *eudaimonia*. We can't all be good at everything. Don't try to be what you aren't. Our genes do define us to a degree. We may wish that we had been born more beautiful, or cleverer, or more athletic. We may think that life would have been different if we had been born into another strata of society, and it probably would. The only solution to that, however, is the advice that my barber gave me when I asked what to do about my increasing baldness: 'You should have changed your parents before you were born,' he said. And I would never have wanted that.

'Know Yourself' was, Juvenal tells us, one of the messages inscribed on the temple of Apollo in Delphi in Ancient Greece. Difficult. But the corollary, 'Accept Yourself', is just as difficult. Like many people, I suppose, I can imagine a different life if I had been born different, had a different upbringing or a more testing early life. I have to live with the face I see in that mirror, screw it every which way though I may. It's all very well for Aristotle to suggest that we concentrate on what we do best, but knowing what that is and then settling for it is another matter.

It is particularly difficult if what you do best can only be done when you were younger. I recall interviewing for some radio programme the manager of the Wigan rugby league team, at that time the league champions.

'What is your biggest challenge?' I asked him. His reply surprised me.

'It is persuading the young lions in my team that their playing days will be over before they are thirty and coaxing them to retrain for another career.'

What those young men did best they can't do for very long. It is the same for all athletes whose best years will soon be behind them and for whom the rest of life could well be an anticlimax. It is only a little better, because later, for those whose skill lies in managing others. Unless they are lucky their organisations will want to ease them out while, in their eyes, they are still in their prime. Discovering another version of one's best in so-called retirement can be hard. Shell told me when I joined them that most of their executives died within eighteen months after retiring. For them there was no *eudaimonia* after Shell. Professionals can fare better if they can base an independent life around their professional skills. This gets harder, however, as more and more professions require one to take out expensive insurance in order to continue to practise their trade, and when keeping oneself up to date in the changing technology can be challenging as well as costly.

We are having to reinvent retirement, now that it can last for twenty, even thirty years, most of them healthy ones. Retirement is obviously the wrong word. It is another stage of life, an unexpected bonus of prosperity. We would be crazy not to take advantage of it. One of the books that Elizabeth and I did together was called *Reinvented Lives*. In it twenty-eight women wrote about what their lives were like in their sixties. With more time now, the children gone, the parents dead, they were free to concentrate on their own lives. Some started new careers, a restaurant with her daughter for one, an international legal consultancy for another, an animal charity for a third. One decided to have the fun with her girlfriends that she had missed out on by marrying young. A couple were happily consumed with grandchildren. One got married for the first time, another for the second. Others had the time now to concentrate more on what they had always done in the gaps in their time and saw their work blossom as a result.

The common factor in all these stories was the way they had each taken positive steps to make the most of these bonus years. They were busy, fulfilled people, living examples of *eudaimonia*. None of them used the word retirement – with one exception, a woman who complained that she had been forcibly retired by her firm. Retirement to her was something that was done to her, not something she chose, although, as she looked back, it was the best thing that could have happened since it propelled her into a new and more interesting life. In time, I suspect, many will look back on their years of formal work as we now look back on our college days, as a long past, formative experience. I asked a neighbour not so long ago to tell me what a mutual acquaintance used to do or be so that I could put some sort of label on him. 'I haven't the faintest idea,' he said, 'it doesn't seem relevant.' The man in question was only sixty-five. It's already happening, I told myself. Men, too, are reinventing themselves in their sixties. I note friends who have bought vineyards, or who have taken up skiing or long-distance walking and made them their new passions. Others have returned to their studies, using Britain's Open University to study what they missed out on in their youth. Many turn artists and reveal a hith-erto unseen talent, or write that novel that we all believe lies some-where within us. Ask them what they used to do and they pass it off with a shrug, something that was important once but now no longer defines them. Their new life is more important now. Without some of the constraints of parenthood and a formal career they are free to concentrate on doing well what they now do best. They have found *eudaimonia* and it shows in their faces. We should all be so fortunate. We could be.

As for me, I am like my farmer friend. Well into his seventies I asked him what he was doing now. 'The same only slower,' he replied. 'Why would I do anything different? It's what I love.' Me too. I liked the story that James O'Toole, my interpreter of Aristotle, tells about John Jerome. Jerome was the author of eleven books; however, when he died in early 2002, his passing went largely unnoticed even in literary and publishing circles. His work had never received much public recognition during his life despite the fact that his meditations on such topics as swimming, mountains, the weather and building a stone wall were thoughtful and well crafted. According to his brother-in-law, *New Yorker* writer Bruce McCall, Jerome had once been bothered by his lack of financial and critical success, until he realised that the purpose of his writing was the pleasure he derived from the act itself.

'Writing his books indeed seemed almost to become John's compensation for not selling books, until one had almost no relation to the other and he was free to turn his writing to the purest purpose of all: to explain the world he lived in to himself.'

My publishers might not want me to be so unaware of my readers, but at heart I now write to explain things to myself, hoping that might interest some readers as well. That earlier ambition to get on the bestseller list has now eased, although I am still vain enough to be chuffed if any book gets there. I am a wordsmith. That's what I do. Looking back, I reinvented my life as I approached fifty and I don't yet feel the need to do it again so radically. The books and articles may change their nature and appear less frequently, the lectures get shorter and more occasional but it will, like my farmer, be the same only slower now. That will leave more time for improving my culinary skills, for eating and talking with my family and friends, for theatres, operas and concerts, other ways of learning because I know, from watching others, that once you stop learning you might as well stop living. None of this will change the world or any part of it, but I long ago embraced that part of the Hippocratic Oath, swearing to myself 'above all, to do no harm'.

Money will always be a concern. Writers have no occupational pensions to collect, only their savings. This is when I envy those who stayed the course in Shell and other organisations, with that inflation-proofed cheque falling into their bank accounts each month with no need to do anything now to earn it, although their successors may not be so well treated. Most people will in future find that they will both need and want to do some money-earning work to supplement whatever pension the state or their past employers will provide. On the other hand, our financial needs do get less as we grow older. Whatever portfolio of activities we create, some of it should earn money. Apart from the practical usefulness of money, it does provide some reassurance that you still have some value to offer.

As I lay in bed I realised once again how fleeting life is, how inconsequential are all our officious strivings, but yet how precious are some parts of it. On balance, I realised life had been kind to me. Loving parents to set me up, wonderful children, a wife whom I adored and to whom I owed any success that I might have achieved, good friends and good health (so far!). To spend the last bit of it doing what I love surrounded by those I love, must be a bonus. I should not need to be cynical. Erich Fromm, the great post-Freudian psychologist, concluded that, despite its difficulties, 'Love is the only sane and satisfactory answer to the problem of existence.' Most of us set out with high hopes and ambitions, determined, as I was, to leave our footprints in the sands of time, only to settle in the end, like Voltaire's Candide, for cultivating our garden. Voltaire also said, 'How infinitesimal is the importance of anything I do, but how infinitely important it is that I do it.' Exactly. I lay back in bed, content.